Earthbound

Ecology and Justice

An Orbis Series on Integral Ecology

Advisory Board Members
Mary Evelyn Tucker
John A. Grim
Leonardo Boff
Sean McDonagh

The Orbis Series on Integral Ecology publishes books seeking to integrate an understanding of Earth's interconnected life systems with sustainable social, political, and economic systems that enhance the Earth community. Books in the series concentrate on ways to

- Reexamine human-Earth relations in light of contemporary cosmological and ecological science.
- Develop visions of common life marked by ecological integrity and social justice.
- Expand on the work of those exploring such fields as integral ecology, climate justice, Earth law, ecofeminism, and animal protection.
- Promote inclusive participatory strategies that enhance the struggle of Earth's poor and oppressed for ecological justice.
- Deepen appreciation for dialogue within and among religious traditions on issues of ecology and justice.
- Encourage spiritual discipline, social engagement, and the transformation of religion and society toward these ends.

Viewing the present moment as a time for fresh creativity and inspired by the encyclical *Laudato Si'*, the series seeks authors who speak to ecojustice concerns and who bring into this dialogue perspectives from the Christian communities, from the world's religions, from secular and scientific circles, or from new paradigms of thought and action.

ECOLOGY AND JUSTICE

Earthbound

God at the Intersection of Climate and Justice

GRACE JI-SUN KIM

ORBIS BOOKS
Maryknoll, New York 10545

Founded in 1970, Orbis Books endeavors to publish works that enlighten the mind, nourish the spirit, and challenge the conscience. The publishing arm of the Maryknoll Fathers and Brothers, Orbis seeks to explore the global dimensions of the Christian faith and mission, to invite dialogue with diverse cultures and religious traditions, and to serve the cause of reconciliation and peace. The books published reflect the views of their authors and do not represent the official position of the Maryknoll Society. To learn more about Maryknoll and Orbis Books, please visit our website at www.orbisbooks.com.

Copyright © 2025 by Grace Ji-Sun Kim.

Published by Orbis Books, Box 302, Maryknoll, NY 10545-0302.

All rights reserved.

No part of this publication may be reproduced or transmitted in any form or by any means, electronic or mechanical, including photocopying, recording, or any information storage or retrieval system, without prior permission in writing from the publisher.

Queries regarding rights and permissions should be addressed to: Orbis Books, P.O. Box 302, Maryknoll, NY 10545-0302.

Manufactured in the United States of America.
Manuscript editing and typesetting by Joan Weber Laflamme.

Library of Congress Cataloging-in-Publication Data

Names: Kim, Grace Ji-Sun, 1969– author.
Title: Earthbound : God at the intersection of climate and justice / Grace Ji-Sun Kim.
Description: Maryknoll, NY : Orbis Books, [2025] | Series: Ecology and justice, an Orbis series on integral ecology | Summary: "Addresses Christian theology, spirituality, and action for environmental justice"— Provided by publisher.
Identifiers: LCCN 2025005069 (print) | LCCN 2025005070 (ebook) | ISBN 9781626986312 (trade paperback) | ISBN 9798888660867 (epub)
Subjects: LCSH: Ecotheology. | Climatic changes. | Environmental justice—Religious aspects—Christianity.
Classification: LCC BT695.5 .K56 2025 (print) | LCC BT695.5 (ebook)| DDC 261.8/8—dc23/eng/20250212
LC record available at https://lccn.loc.gov/2025005069
LC ebook record available at https://lccn.loc.gov/2025005070

To my lovely nephew and niece,
Matthew and Naomi

Contents

Acknowledgments 9

Introduction 11
    The Problem 12
    A Way Forward 16

1. Living Water 19
    Water for Life 19
    Water Distribution 23
    Commodification of Water 25
    Virtual Water 27
    Water and Faith Communities 28
    World Council of Churches and Water
      Justice 30
    Water Protectors 34
    Baptism 35
    Discussion Questions 39

2. Intersecting Injustices 41
    Economic Injustice 42
    Climate Refugees 51
    Gender Injustice 54
    Environmental Racism 61
    Discussion Questions 67

3. Exploring Theology at the Intersection of Climate and Justice — 69
    Christian Misinterpretations, Misbehaviors, and Mistakes   72
    Christianity Must Reimagine a Better World   74
    Contextual Theology and Climate Justice   85
    Discussion Questions   98

4. God Is a Verb — 99
    A Dynamic God   100
    A Loving God   112
    God the Loving, Dynamic Spirit   116
    Discussion Questions   127

5. Living with Hope — 129
    Sin and *Han*   130
    Dandelions Are Good   135
    Flourishing   137
    Loving Our Neighbors   138
    Peacemaking   140
    Hoping   141
    Discussion Questions   142

Conclusion   143

Acknowledgments

Climate justice is not an individual endeavor. It is a collective, communal effort that thrives through the engagement of churches, faith communities, and countless dedicated individuals. Over the years I have had the privilege of being part of the World Council of Churches working group on climate change, where I have participated in COP (Conference of the Parties) meetings and collaborated with other faith-based organizations, including GreenFaith, the Tzu Chi Foundation, Religions for Peace, and many others. I am deeply grateful to these organizations for their unwavering commitment to inspiring people of faith to advocate for climate justice, and for pressuring governments, church leaders, and corporations to take meaningful action. My work has been shaped and sustained by the encouragement of my colleagues and friends, who remind me daily that this fight is for the future of our children and their children.

I am also indebted to the ecofeminist theologians whose pioneering work has paved the way for me to engage in the intersection of sustainability and eco-justice. Their thought leadership has been a source of inspiration, and it is my hope that this book, in its small way, will contribute to the larger, urgent task of protecting God's creation and nurturing a sustainable future for our planet. I am also thankful to friends Cara Highsmith, Janice Laidlaw, Hilda Koster, and Susan Shaw for their support and kindness.

My sincere gratitude goes to publisher Robert Ellsberg, whose encouragement led me to submit the *Earthbound* manuscript to Orbis Books. Robert's dedication to the field of faith-based publishing is unparalleled, and it is truly an honor to publish my second book with Orbis. I am equally grateful to Dr. Thomas Hermans-Webster, whose meticulous editing and theological insight strengthened this manuscript. His careful attention to detail helped transform my work into what it is today, and I am deeply appreciative of his expertise and guidance. I am also thankful to the entire team at Orbis Books for its professionalism and support throughout the publishing process.

As always, I owe a debt of gratitude to my family, whose unwavering support makes this work possible. To my spouse, Perry, and our three children, Theo, Elisabeth, and Joshua, thank you for your patience, encouragement, and love throughout this journey. I am also deeply grateful to my extended family for their kindness and generosity, and to my nephew Matthew and niece Naomi for their ongoing support in countless ways. To all the family and friends who continue to believe in my work, I am forever thankful.

This book is a testament to the collective efforts of many, and it would not have been possible without the love, faith, and dedication of so many people. Thank you.

Introduction

We are interrelated and interdependent. Humans and other animals, plants, water, air, soils, and atoms live together in a common home, Earth. Each of us influences and affects others, and these relationships cascade across ecosystems, bioregions, watersheds, continents, and oceans. We know that there are connections between our actions and how our world functions, and a lot of people want to find ways to make a sustainable, clean, and flourishing world so that our children can survive and thrive. Yet the sheer magnitude of our relationships can overwhelm us when we witness our fellow creatures and our very Earth suffering.

Our relationships intersect in so many ways, and they help make us who we are. Some of these are intersections of identity, like gender and race; others are intersections of class affiliation, religious life, or educational background. As each of us becomes more aware of our relational influences, we can begin to feel a sense of responsibility to other people, other creatures, and our environments. This book is about that responsibility.

I am a Christian theologian, and this book is a Christian theological reflection on life and God that engages overlapping concerns for the well-being of our world, including climate change, water health, and environmental racism. Whether you are Christian or not, I hope this book can help you reflect on how you have been influenced by and are influencing whole worlds of life. How we relate to one another, including other creatures and our environments, can cause great harm to our world. It can also be a source for healing justice, transforming love, and flourishing creativity. Together, we can act in love for one another and God's creation.

The Problem

Climate change is happening right before our eyes. We can pretend that it is no big deal or that it is an alarmist idea, but we cannot ignore the devastation that has occurred from the growing climate crisis. Scientists from various countries and fields of study have been warning the public for years that we must change our policies and practices if we are to avert disaster or, at least, mitigate the worst possible effects. Now, many of them warn us that we do not have much time to halt the destruction if we even have time left at all. Extreme weather events, including droughts, hurricanes, monsoons, and tornadoes, are worsening and affect all of us on the planet.

This is more than a few extra degrees on the average thermometer and longer summer seasons. Changing climates affect habitats for all sorts of creatures on land and in the sea; food sources that are or are not available to creatures in evolutionarily expected seasons; plant growth, from photosynthesis rates for oxygen production to fruit and vegetable produce for human communities. These effects have an adverse impact upon human food security, life expectancy, education, and health, to name just a few aspects of our lives. Climate changes are even producing climate refugees: people whose homelands are no longer livable because of increasingly compounding factors like drought, flooding, erosion, famine, blight, and disease.

We have come to this stage not by a random act but by conscious decisions to repeatedly abuse our use of fossil fuels, particularly coal and oil. Our fossil-fuel use has, in the past one hundred and fifty years, "dramatically increased" carbon dioxide amounts in our atmosphere to the highest levels in about three million years![1] Our fossil-fuel abuse is part of a larger pattern of extraction and degradation that includes clear-cutting forests; pumping chemical waste into the air, soil, and water; strip mining; and depleting farmlands, forests, and oceans of life-sustaining and life-producing webs of relational creatures.

We have subscribed to the fallacy that we can take anything from Earth while Earth will naturally replenish itself. "Greenhouse gases like carbon dioxide and methane trap heat and drive global warming," and the tremendous increase in their emissions could "tip the earth into a hothouse state, beyond our ability to intervene if we don't interrupt current trends."[2] We have failed to fundamentally understand that Earth cannot restore its resources and keep up with the rate at which we consume them.

As much as we have been told to claim individual responsibility by not littering, recycling, and making healthier food choices, big corporations and ultra-wealthy persons are polluting and damaging the earth at an alarming rate that far surpasses most regular people. Both individuals

---

[1] Simon Orpana, *Gasoline Dreams: Waking Up from Petroculture* (New York: Fordham University Press, 2021), 8.

[2] Orpana, 8–9.

and corporations are at fault, and both contribute to pollution. Greed drives their decisions because their decisions are focused on the extraction of resources for the accumulation of wealth. They bear the greatest share of responsibility for what is happening to our climate. I am not the first to make this argument, and I will not be the last. The challenges we face are not just technological; they are cultural, even theological.

Fossil-fuel use is a major cultural practice, and it is the single most significant cultural practice contributing to climate change. Fossil fuels are formed from the decomposition of buried carbon-based organisms that died millions of years ago. They create carbon-rich deposits that are extracted and burned for energy. The burning of fossil fuels refers to the burning of oil, natural gas, and coal to generate energy. We use this energy to generate electricity and to power transportation and industrial processes. Nearly all human societies on our planet are being sourced by the energy produced by burning fossil fuels.

The emissions from burning fossil fuels include carbon dioxide and methane, both powerful greenhouse gases. These greenhouse gases then trap heat in our atmosphere, which causes warming temperatures at various rates around the planet.[3] Greenhouse-gas emissions from the burning of fossil fuels are having far-reaching effects on our climate and ecosystems and will lead to self-destruction as the ecosystem overloads.[4]

---

[3] "Fossil Fuels and Climate Change: The Facts," *ClientEarth* online, February 18, 2022.

[4] "Understanding Global Change," A Project of The University of California Museum of Paleontology online (Berkeley: University of California, 2023).

In addition to ecological-justice concerns and climate change, fossil-fuel extraction, use, and abuse are directly connected to economic and social justice issues. Since the invention of coal-fired steam engines of the 1700s, our burning of fossil fuels has dramatically increased and has contributed to rapid industrialization, individualist capitalism, and tremendous wealth inequality. "In the western world, and North America in particular, we have become energy vampires, sucking up more than our fair share of energy resources in pursuit of lifestyles that rarely deliver on the promises of prosperity and happiness that are sold to us."[5] To create comfortable lifestyles, we are destroying Earth's health and threatening the viability of all creatures, great and small. We have become so entrenched in cultures of fossil-fuel consumption that it is hard for us to comprehend how burning fossil fuels frees us to live comfortably and travel seemingly anywhere we could want while it also destroys the very lives, ecosystems, bioregions, and planet where we want to live well.

Simply put, the extent of the destruction will lead to mass death. As we continue to emit toxins into the air, soil, and water, we must ask ourselves how much longer we are willing to kill one another. We must commit to taking restorative steps to care for Earth, our home, so it can sustain life for many generations to come.[6]

Because ecological justice is so intimately connected to economic and social justice, we are currently faced with two important challenges: lifting up the lives of the global poor, and stabilizing the earth's climate so that it will stop

---

[5] Orpana, *Gasoline Dreams*, 51.
[6] Grace Ji-Sun Kim and Naomi Faith Bu, "Rescuing Home: Climate Change and COP21," *Huffington Post*, December 21, 2015.

warming. The way we confront and tackle these challenges will determine our quality of life today and in years to come.[7] As participants in an interrelated world, our actions affect the lives of everyone around the world and vice versa. From knowing that how we live will affect so many around the world, we can pivot toward meaningful acts of climate justice in our own contexts.

A Way Forward

For the sake of creation, of our siblings in the human family and the earth family, of our planet, and of ourselves, we need to work together for environmental justice, and we need to fight to reverse the damage that our actions have caused. While we cannot ignore the insights and warnings from climate and earth sciences, we need to recognize the vital cultural and theological changes that must take place to restore our relationships in our common home. How we understand and relate to humanity and God influence and are influenced by our broader social and cultural attitudes. Changes to lifestyles, outlooks, and theologies on personal levels can help turn our path around as a church and a society so that we can be on a journey to save Earth. We must admit that we do not own the land. As Indigenous spiritualities often reflect, we borrow or are woven within the land and its rich web of life. Within these relationships, we can understand that the crises we are experiencing are not due to animals, plants, the sun, or the wind.

Human beings, particularly in European and North American contexts, have decided to live and interact with

---

[7] Kim and Bu, 10.

this planet in unsustainable ways, extracting and degrading life all around us. We are responsible, and we must take ownership of this problem. We need to stop our careless disregard for our common home before our actions do even more irreversible damage to Earth. The work is immense, but, if we all participate in it, we can make progress in mending the problems we have created. We must work toward climate justice if we are going to survive as a people and a planet.

Importantly for this book, we must rethink our understanding and images of God in light of climate justice. In the chapters that follow we look at the issue of water and how contamination and waste are both major ways that our behaviors influence the health of water worldwide. We consider the intersection of racial, gender, and economic injustice in relationship to the climate and environmental conditions of our planet. There are profound imbalances in our relational systems that highlight the ongoing disregard we hold for our fellow creatures. We explore how our understanding and images of God directly influence how we experience, think about, and act within the world. Theologies that prioritize God as domineering, supreme, or a king lead to a patriarchal worldview and have been used to legitimize human dominance over other creatures and structures of dominance within human communities, such as patriarchy, racism, and heterosexism. Doing theology that takes climate justice seriously can help prevent further climate crises and heal our hurting world.

Theologically, we must shift our priorities to experiencing God as active with us, moving us to work for justice and helping us to heal the earth. This will be a theology of verbs, action words that can revive our relationships with

God, one another, and creation, motivating us in our aim to stabilize and heal our planet. Finally, we will position ourselves in hope for the work to be done and the possibilities for healing Earth with God and one another.

1

Living Water

Water for Life

We need water to live.[1] Water runs through all living things, keeping us alive and well in our shared earthly home. In mighty rivers and gentle streams, it flows through Earth's diverse and dynamic ecosystems. It sustains us, heals us, and gives us life. For Christians, the waters of baptism both weave us into the body of Christ and bring the whole creation into God's saving love in our lives. Yet, we have poisoned our waterways and polluted our oceans and lakes with the waste that we have produced. We need water to live, and, if we continue to contaminate our sources of water and do nothing to clean it up and prevent further pollution, we will be the end of humanity and our creaturely kin on Earth.

When we think about how struggles for social justice interact with climate change concerns, water may be the most important topic for our work. The ocean contains 97 percent of the earth's water. Ocean habitats support

---

[1] Grace Ji-Sun Kim, "Climate Justice Is for All: Making Peace with the Earth," in *Gathered in My Name: Ecumenism in the World Church*, ed. William T. Cavanaugh (Eugene, OR: Cascade, 2020), 144.

countless creatures, from shallow tide pools to depths too great for sunlight. Very little of the earth's water is the fresh water that a lot of land creatures, including ourselves, need to live. Even when all the rivers, ponds, and lakes of the world are counted together, fresh water is precious, limited, and vulnerable.

Water and climate are intertwined, of course. From multiple factors, our water supply is influenced by this present climate crisis. Changes in water—like temperature, salt levels, nitrogen levels, and oxygen levels—are some of the fundamental indicators of the extent of climate change. For example, as greenhouse gases exponentially accumulate in the atmosphere, the temperature of the air rises, increasing the temperatures of the ocean. The ocean will continue to warm, with devastating impacts on sea life and that ecosystem.[2] This warming, in turn, causes glaciers to melt and sea levels to rise. The melting ice also changes the salt levels and destabilizes food webs in the ocean and beyond. On land, the greenhouse effect contributes to mountain snowpacks melting, which means that snow does not stay as long as it used to after winter at higher elevations. The runoff from the melting snow might not be enough water to fill our springs and rivers in the springtime, and the streams of meltwater dry up sooner in the late spring and early summer. Additionally, increasing surface temperatures are projected to lengthen heat waves, which will also occur more often. This will also lead to more extreme precipitation events in some areas because warmer air can hold more moisture,

---

[2] Elizabeth McAnally, *Loving Water across Religions: Contributions to an Integral Water Ethic* (Maryknoll, NY: Orbis Books, 2019), 13.

increasing flooding risks from storms like hurricanes, monsoons, and typhoons.

Though the glaciers and large sheet ice covering Greenland and Antarctica do contribute to the increase of sea levels as they start to melt, thermal expansion of seawater is the primary cause of increasing sea levels. As liquid warms, it takes up more space. Sea levels have risen roughly twenty centimeters since the late 1800s, and the rate of rise appears to have increased in recent decades. With the highest tides and the surges of waves during major storms, sea-level rise, especially an increasing rate of rise, is dangerous to so many of the world's population who live close to or at sea level. Even a half-meter rise will have serious consequences in places such as Bangladesh that do not have the resources and infrastructure to adapt to rising sea levels. As the sea level continues to rise, people will lose their homes and their ways of life, which will contribute to an increase of climate refugees and migrants.

Oceans around the world are also heavily polluted with trash. Some of this pollution is illegally dumped or accidentally spilled into the ocean from ships or offshore oil rigs. Furthermore, "virtually every kind of plastic packaging and plastic object used on land may be discarded or lost to the sea."[3] There are five major ocean gyres, where currents converge. The North Pacific Gyre holds within it the Great Pacific Garbage Patch (also called the Pacific Trash Vortex). The Great Pacific Garbage Patch "spans waters from the West Coast of North America to Japan. The

---

[3] Robert H. Day et al., *Quantitative Distribution and Characteristics of Neustonic Plastic in the North Pacific Ocean: Final Report to US Department of Commerce, National Marine Fisheries Service*, Auke Bay Laboratory (1998), 247–66.

patch is actually comprised of the Western Garbage Patch, located near Japan, and the Eastern Garbage Patch, located between the US states of Hawai'i and California."[4] This soup of garbage is composed of a vast variety of debris, including fishing nets, single-use plastic bags, toothbrushes, shoes, boat scraps, and pre-production microplastic resin pellets called nurdles.

Approximately 80 percent of the pollution in the Great Pacific Garbage Patch comes from activities that occur on land in North America and Asia.[5] This garbage patch greatly affects marine life, including plants, fish, mammals, and birds. It is a powerful result of how intersecting injustices within human communities affect all of life, including human beings.

Cleaning up and protecting our oceans, seas, lakes, and other waterways is not about fulfilling some European colonial vision of neat and tidy "beauty." Oil and natural-gas pipelines transport fossil fuels from extraction sites to refineries, often on river and ocean shorelines. The pipelines eventually leak the toxic oil and gas along their routes, poisoning water supplies and irreparably damaging soil, plant, and animal health.[6] The Garbage Patch, like other polluting runoffs and spills, is a result of economic exploitation. Wealthier nations overconsume goods that are often intentionally disposable, creating untold amounts of waste. Corporations, seeking to increase their profits, both encourage waste-creating overconsumption and establish

---

[4] "Great Pacific Garbage Patch," *National Geographic: Education*, https://education.nationalgeographic.org/resource/great-pacific-garbage-patch/ (updated October 31, 2024).

[5] McAnally, *Loving Water across Religions*, 12.

[6] Kim, "Climate Justice Is for All," 147.

manufacturing centers in places where they can exploit laborers in the name of "saving manufacturing costs." Often, these laborers are women and migrants. The urgent calls to pursue healthy water systems in a healed climate cannot be separated from the Christian care for the poor and our pursuit of Jubilee justice.

Water Distribution

Our current water crisis has many causes, aspects, and impacts. Climate science may seem so big a picture that it can be overwhelming, and the reality of masses of garbage that are larger than Texas floating in the ocean might be hard to comprehend, let alone engage. On a more local level, the availability of clean water for drinking, basic hygiene, and ecosystem health is an increasing problem. The distribution of clean, fresh water is a central justice issue. While we each need to think about and understand our own water uses, we must also create systems of justice that distribute water without reinforcing today's economic, racial, and gender-based oppressions. We must reimagine the ways we use and share water to do what we need to do.[7]

Many people around the world do not have access to clean drinking water. This problem often emerges along wealth lines and other markers of identity within countries. Water access concerns do not neatly fit into old colonial titles of "developed" and "developing" countries. One-in-three people around the world do not have access to safe drinking water. This means that billions of people around the world are continuing to suffer from

---

[7] Kim, 144.

poor sanitation and hygiene.[8] The United Nations has reported that 1.1 billion people do not have safe water to drink, and 2.6 billion people suffer from inadequate sewerage.[9] Children are the most vulnerable victims of the water crisis, and many die every year from contaminated water and improper sanitation. Polluted water leads to health issues, climate justice issues, political issues, and economic issues.[10] And since all plant life needs water to grow and thrive, access to adequate clean water ripples outward and influences agriculture, food production, and the livelihood of those who work to provide food for us all. Water access is a social justice issue of multiple dimensions. These issues are all interrelated, and we must tackle them together.

Having access to clean water is a basic human right, yet the manufactured scarcity of clean water creates a distribution imbalance that favors people and communities who will pay—in money, labor, and time—the costs to "win" a scarce resource. For communities who will not or cannot pay, their access to clean water will diminish while their experiences of contamination will increase. In changing climates our water concerns will intensify. Droughts and flooding alike change how and where water moves in our

---

[8] "1 in 3 People Globally Do Not Have Access to Safe Drinking Water—UNICEF, WHO," *World Health Organization*, June 19, 2019.

[9] "No Child Should Have to Drink Dirty Water," UNICEF, March 19, 2021.

[10] The World Health Organization (WHO) says that almost two billion people drink water that is contaminated with feces, which puts them at risk for cholera, typhoid, and polio. Haruna Kashiwase and Tony Fujs, "World Water Day: Two Billion People Still Lack Access to Safely Managed Water," in *World Bank Blogs*, March 22, 2023.

world. Both extremes, occurring more frequently and more dramatically, will create health crises and significantly damage our existing infrastructure for distribution.

Commodification of Water

When clean water is distributed and limited as a scarce resource, it can be turned into a profitable commodity. As a commodity, water becomes sold, bought, owned, hoarded, and withheld. Gone are common assumptions that just drinking tap water is considered safe enough without extra filters. When I was growing up in the 1970s and 1980s, we also drank from the water fountains or garden hoses without much care. However, in just one generation, the commodification of water has fueled a billion-dollar bottled water industry just to provide this life-giving resource, which most Americans can get from the tap.

Bottles, jugs, and dispensers separate us from water and from one another. On the straight road for the mass commodification of water, communities lose their water sources while fossil-fuel corporations extract and burn even more fuel to create bottle after bottle. Once bottled, the water gets sold back to those communities at higher prices than they would have paid through a municipal water utility. The water-bottle industry uses millions of barrels of oil to produce and ship plastic water bottles around the United States and the world. The plastic water bottles are then discarded, eventually littering the oceans, lakes, and rivers as deadly traps for marine life.

For centuries communities relied on free-flowing rivers and streams as sources of water for their well-being, including daily living needs and agriculture. Now, water is offered for sale to the highest bidder. In the absence of protective laws, favor goes to industry and those with deep pockets, and the average person inevitably suffers. As has happened in every generation of our settler-colonial nation's history, wealthy land developers claim and consume everything they can get their hands on, whether they have ownership of it or not. Communities of color, Native American tribes, and poor communities bear the brunt of this water theft.

Commodifying water goes against everything that God stands for in the creation of the world—the freeness of God's bounty and beauty for all of God's creation. Our world is a gift so that all could survive and flourish. In 2023, the global water industry's market was $342.4 billion, and about fifty billion bottles of water were purchased just in the United States. The bottled water market continues to grow, and it is projected to increase by 5.24 percent through 2027. The profit margin for these companies is a whopping 50 percent to 200 percent.[11] This incredible profit margin would have been unimaginable a couple of generations ago.

Withholding water, creating a scarcity through greed, and exploiting that scarcity as a source of power over others is anti-Christ. Churches must advocate for an end to selling God's creation for personal profit. We must recognize our human responsibility to care for, not to dominate

---

[11] Alvin Juline, "The 10 Largest Bottled Water Companies in the World," *Zippia* online, April 4, 2023.

and pilfer, creation. To overcome our greed and desire to use creation for profit, we must recognize the holiness of creation. To recognize the holiness of creation, we must recognize God's creation as part of God's body.

Virtual Water

The commodification of water has hidden, or virtual, costs. Water is commodified beyond bottling and selling drinking water. Often we fail to discuss these virtual costs because they have been hidden in other systems of commodification, especially food and agricultural systems. The true costs of our food include setting groceries and other foods at low prices that can only be economically justified by the inhumane exploitation of laborers, animals, and environmental sources like soil and water. Virtual water is more than the actual water we use to drink and clean. For example, taking a ten-minute shower may require thirty-two gallons of water; a burger requires about 530 gallons of water, and that's before any bun, cheese, lettuce, tomato, or bacon toppings. The virtual water that we consume in an average hamburger only includes the amount that is required to raise, feed, slaughter, and process the cow.

The world wastes about 2.5 billion tons of food each year, and nearly 60 million tons of that waste is produced in the United States; this is equal to about 40 percent of the US food supply or 325 pounds of waste per individual per year.[12] Hunger is not for lack of food supply. Rather, hunger is a policy choice. Community, state, and

---

[12] "Food Waste in America in 2025," *Recycle Track Systems*.

federal policymakers prioritize keeping a segment of the population hungry and food insecure in order to inflate the shareholder profits for food corporations, especially the "Big 10."[13] When policymakers choose to allow hunger and food insecurity to exist apart from the true amount of food supply in the country, food waste is also a policy choice. People go to bed hungry, but not because there isn't enough food. Water, soil, labor, animals' lives, and entire ecosystems are wasted because food and water are used for financial efficiency and profits instead of community health and well-being.

When we calculate the virtual water for the foods we consume and the foods we waste, we come to realize that we are wasting much more water than we drink. In addition to thinking about creation justice, Christian concern for justice in water use must consider how our meals affect the quality and availability of water in our communities, our nation, and our world. If we want to move toward living sustainably as sharers of Earth's water, then we must rethink our diets and foodways, prioritizing foods and practices that require less virtual water.

Water and Faith Communities

As some Protestant churches around the world celebrate five hundred years since the Reformation, many are wondering how we can continue to reform the church, continue

---

[13] Nestlé, Coca-Cola, Unilever, Danone, Mars, Mondelez, Associated British Foods, Kellogg's, General Mills, and Pepsico own the vast majority of the various food brands in international markets.

to make a difference in people's lives, and continue to have a positive influence on the world. One important question among the churches during this five hundredth anniversary is how the churches deal with sustainability and climate change. Caroline Bader, a former youth secretary of the Lutheran World Federation, has directly tied the reforming spirit to protection of and justice for creation. Expanding Luther's emphasis on God's love freely available to all, she talked about how "one of our thematic approaches to the commemoration of five hundred years of Lutheran Reformation is the theme 'Creation—Not for Sale.'"[14] Framing Christian efforts to protect and relate to creation through God's redeeming love also reframes our relationships to people who suffer critical environmental challenges as a result of climate change. Specifically concerning water, Christian communities have a baptismal connection to clean, safe, and lifegiving fresh water. Baptismal waters tie Christians to the waters of all creation, and God's redeeming love is made known to each of us in both. When water and land are closed off from communal enjoyment and benefit, sold away to the highest bidder, or leased for extraction, we can recognize and resist greed as a sin that gets in the way of God's love. That greed jeopardizes our right relationships with God and our neighbors, including all of creation.[15]

In the face of environmental sin and its destructive consequences, churches must advocate for climate justice and work toward a greener future that encourages sustainable

---

[14] "Creation—Not for Sale," Twelfth Assembly, The Lutheran World Federation, Windhoek, Namibia (2017).

[15] Caroline Bader, interview with the author, December 2016.

living. These phrases—climate justice, greener future, and sustainable living—cannot be hollow sayings. Water, as it flows throughout our world, can teach us how to interact with our local environments. You can actually follow the water to find your place of action for climate justice; we all live in a watershed. Your watershed—the rivers, streams, and lakes that collect the rain that falls in your area—can be the local context where you and your church live God's loving justice for creation with faith and courage.

World Council of Churches and Water Justice

At the international level, the World Council of Churches (WCC) working group on climate change includes members from around the world who reflect theologically on climate change, speak out on environmental issues, and advocate for sustainable living. To emphasize the link between environmental justice and economic justice, the WCC has adopted the term *eco-justice* for its approach, implemented across several projects and initiatives. The Ecumenical Water Network of the WCC, for example, emphasizes that access to clean water is a human right.

The WCC founded the Ecumenical Water Network (EWN) in 2008 to advocate for water justice in the Middle East, especially Palestine. Israelis living in illegal settlements in the occupied Palestinian Territories have access to clean water for drinking and sanitation, while Palestinians in Gaza and the West Bank do not.[16] The WCC is one

---

[16] Grace Ji-Sun Kim and Ilkka Sipilainen, "Lack of Water Justice Endangers Peace and Good Life," *The Huffington Post,* December 6, 2017.

of many organizations that is doing its part to speak out against environmental injustices, and they rightly include water access and distribution in the scope of environmental-justice concerns. Many Christian churches around the world understand climate justice as broadly configured to include racial justice, gender justice, and human rights protections.

On July 28, 2010, through Resolution 64/294, the United Nations General Assembly explicitly recognized the human right to water and sanitation, acknowledging that clean drinking water and sanitation are essential to the realization of all human rights. The resolution called upon states and international organizations to provide financial resources, capacity building, and technology transfer to help countries, in particular developing countries, to provide safe, clean, accessible, and affordable drinking water and sanitation for their citizens.[17]

Access to clean water is a cause of conflict in many places in our world, thrusting water justice to the top of Christian priorities for peace. While some Christians continue to argue about the causes of climate change against the very convincing results of climate sciences, no person can deny the human need for water and the moral priority for safe access to it without also denying the Christian moral commitment to the common good.

When access to clean water is not available to all, the deterioration of society follows.[18] Polluted water provides an environment for waterborne diseases such as cholera, contributes to skin and digestion issues, and can lead to

---

[17] Kim, "Climate Justice Is for All," 146.
[18] Kim, 146.

death.[19] One example of water-access issues that is directly connected to the WCC's Ecumenical Water Network is the distribution of clean water in Israel and Palestine even before October 7, 2023.

Before the Israeli airstrikes against Gaza in October 2023, the state of clean water availability in Gaza and the West Bank was already dire. Israelis living in illegal settlements in the occupied Palestinian Territories have had total access to clean drinking water, while Palestinians have either lacked access to clean water or have lived with access so limited that they precariously face water insecurity. There has been a constant struggle for equitable water distribution so that those in the occupied territories have the same access, per capita, to clean water as Israel does.[20] Because they hold the political and military power in the region, Israelis have been able to turn entire water supply systems off and on, depriving Palestinians of water access and using water access as a leverage point to increase Israeli power. This control violates Palestinians' basic human rights, but major international forces, primarily the United States, have failed to hold Israel accountable for these violations.

After the October 7, 2023, attack by Hamas, Israel turned off Gaza's water supply as well as severing its electricity supply and its food-supply network. This decision was made to punish Gazan Palestinians in retaliation for the Hamas attack. Following days of international protest, Israel turned back on just some of the water supply to

---

[19] Kim and Sipilainen, "Lack of Water Justice Endangers Peace and Good Life"; Kim, "Climate Justice Is for All," 145.

[20] Kim, "Climate Justice Is for All," 145.

Gaza.[21] The power of an occupier to supply or withhold life support for people is a crime and is morally reprehensible. As a gift from God, water must never be used as a weapon of war. Doing so is a sin that exposes people to tremendous risks for illness, violence, and death.

Settler-colonial violence intersects with concerns for environmental well-being. Part of the Israeli bombing campaigns in Gaza and Lebanon has included the illegal use of white phosphorus. It is being used as a weapon to set fires that burn people and structures regardless of strategic military importance. White phosphorus causes excruciating burns and lifelong suffering if the burn victim survives.[22] In addition to the wildfire danger to an arid ecosystem, using white phosphorus artillery to burn a population that does not have access to water is an atrocity. Even when human communities escape the fire danger, the ecological consequences of both fires and chemical fallout are deadly.

When we pay attention to water, we learn to notice how our whole world is interconnected. The phosphorous acids that result from the volatile exposure of white phosphorus to oxygen can remain and accumulate in soil and water sources over time, increasing the toxicity of waterways. Though contamination may not be immediately apparent, nearby crops, livestock, and wild animals can be threatened

---

[21] Natasha Hall, Anita Kirschenbaum, and David Michel, "The Siege of Gaza's Water," *Center for Strategic and International Studies* online (January 12, 2024).

[22] Alan Arms and Marija Ristic, "Israel/OPT: Identifying the Israeli Army's Use of White Phosphorus in Gaza," *Amnesty International* online (October 13, 2023); Amnesty International, "Lebanon: Evidence of Israel's Unlawful Use of White Phosphorus in Southern Lebanon as Cross-Border Hostilities Escalate," *Amnesty International* online (October 31, 2023).

by the increased levels of the phosphorus acids and elemental phosphorus in their drinking water. War and its fallout are never limited to the humans in combat.

Water Protectors

In some instances we can witness people who want to protect the earth and the water that gives life. Some people do not see water as a commodity to be sold. Rather, water is a natural source of life for all creatures that should be readily available and accessible to everyone. When water protectors act, we must be keen to learn from them and follow their lead.

Recent protest action to stop the construction of the Dakota Access Pipeline is a critical example of water protection today. The Dakota Access Pipeline's route went through four states and was almost twelve-hundred miles in length, from the Bakken oil fields in northwestern North Dakota through South Dakota, Iowa, and Illinois. The pipeline project proposed to cross the Missouri River, just north of the Standing Rock Sioux Reservation in North Dakota. This crossing became a historic place of protest against this pipeline and for the sacred waters. These protestors were called Water Protectors.

The focal point was a fight over how the pipeline's route was analyzed and approved by the federal government. Members of the tribe and their supporters argued that they were not adequately consulted about the route of the pipeline, violating their tribal sovereignty. They made legal challenges and voiced public protests about this specific route. Water Protectors warned that running the pipeline under a Missouri River reservoir called Lake Oahe would jeopardize, and possibly contaminate, the primary water source for the Standing Rock reservation. If the pipes cracked or burst, the water and land would become poisoned. The Dakota Access Pipeline construction would further damage sacred sites near the lake, which would further violate tribal treaty rights.[23]

Water Protectors from Standing Rock are part of an international movement for climate justice that has been largely led by Indigenous Peoples. At the United Nations annual meeting on climate change—Congress of the Parties (COP)—in Marrakech, Water Protectors from Standing Rock bore powerful witness to how water issues are a planetary concern. Whatever happens to the water in the United States will eventually affect the waters in India, South Africa, and Brazil. Water connects us to one another across vast distances and within our intimate communities. As Christians, we have a holy opportunity to experience the wideness of God's love in our world and our lives when we learn from and act with Water Protectors.

Baptism

Christians have a spiritual relationship with water. In the sacrament of baptism, water is necessary. As an outward and visible sign of an inward and spiritual grace, baptism marks how one becomes part of the family of God. In this

---

[23] Rebecca Hersher, "Key Moments in the Dakota Access Pipeline Fight," *NPR: WBEZ Chicago*, February 22, 2017.

perspective the water of the baptismal covenant becomes thicker than the blood of family. In baptism we are publicly claimed within the cloud of witnesses and the body of Christ through the love of God and the power of the Holy Spirit.

The reciprocal and public nature of the ritual deeply challenges the individual and the church community to hold one another with loving accountability and commitment to care. When an adult is baptized, a community of faith may say, "You have now made the decision to declare that you are part of this body called together by Christ." When an infant is baptized, the community may say, "Those who have made the decision on your behalf have brought you into this body called together by Christ." In both infant and adult baptism one becomes connected to others beyond our earthly understandings and joined together with our ancestors, those present with us now, and those to come for eternity.[24]

Baptismal actions show a deeper understanding of who God is and how God connects with us in each and every day through water all around us. Baptism becomes a ritual that allows us to experience the grace and presence of God in the world and in our lives.[25] God uses the waters of baptism to weave our whole selves into God's own life, in gracious love and mercy.

Baptism reminds us of water's vitality for our world and teaches us to seek its lifegiving, cleansing, and refreshing gift. Water is essential for life on Earth and in the "kindom" of God. Just as water cleans the physical body, the

---

[24] Bruce Reyes-Chow, *Everything Good about God Is True* (Minneapolis: Broadleaf Books, 2024), 129.
[25] Reyes-Chow, 126.

Holy Spirit moves through the baptismal waters to clean the soul.[26] Through baptism, God forgives our sins and washes us so that we may heal in Christ's gracious love. Washed in the waters of baptism, we are offered the opportunity to live in the abundant life that Jesus has promised. He called himself Living Water and, to the Samaritan woman at the well, said: "Those who drink of the water that I will give them will never be thirsty. The water that I will give will become in them a spring of water gushing up to eternal life" (Jn 4:14). Our spiritual relationship with water is more than some romanticist commitment to conservation of so-called wild nature. Water links us to our past and moves with us into a future, enlivening our whole world along the way.

Baptism roots us in sacred stories of new beginnings. The biblical story of Noah and the Flood is a story of trying again, recreating and reimagining a world after so much has been lost. The waters are both a destroyer of destruction and the fount through which life pours over all living things. Quenching our thirst and giving new life, water can rush over and trickle through, drip on, and inundate our lives. Yet, it can still be objectified, commodified, and taken for granted when we forget that we must all be protectors of water.

The sacrament of baptism becomes a symbol that all water is sacred, not just the water present in the baptismal font. Because it is sacred, we need to honor water, take care of water, and treat it with holiness, reverence, and love.[27] Through the baptismal waters we begin a faith journey

---

[26] McAnally, *Loving Water across Religions*, 28.
[27] Kaitlin Curtice, *Native: Identity, Belonging and Rediscovering God* (Ada, MI: Brazos Press, 2020), 19.

that awakens us to the beauty of Earth and all of God's creation. We learn that we human beings belong to a community connected to one another through water.[28] We are all made of water and sustained by water. The waters of baptism run through the creeks, rivers, lakes, and oceans of the world, providing life to all living things. Baptism connects Christians to all living things in water's cleansing flows.

In Potawatomi culture women are water protectors. They believe that the water that runs through their bodies is connected to the sacred waters that give sustenance to the lands around us. They remind us that we are one with Earth, not separate from it. We are all part of a planetary organism, so we need each other to survive.[29] Where would we be without the bees who pollinate plants, contributing to the fruits we eat? Where would we be without the water that nourishes the vegetables and animals into flourishing? All of us are necessary within this beautiful creation.

When we remember our baptism, we confront webs of sin and evil that profit from destroying Earth. In these vicious networks financial wealth and political power are valued over and against God's love for life and our community in the body of Christ. Large corporations make billions of dollars by commodifying the earth's gifts, and entire nation-states thrive on wielding power to control humans, other-than-human creatures, and entire ecosystems. When we value financial profit and political power above the covenant of our baptism, we waste the gifts of life in our water, food, and world. When we turn gifts into

---

[28] McAnally, *Loving Water across Religions*, 32.
[29] Curtice, *Native*, 18.

resources and prioritize efficient bottom lines, we pollute our environments and threaten the very health of our baptismal waters. Our relationships with one another, our fellow creatures, and God lose the grace of love when we seek only power and riches.

The good news is that there is another way, a holy way, a loving way. Water is essential to life, and we can live in its beauty and abundance. We can choose life, and we can be encouraged by the Spirit who hovered over the waters in Genesis. We can act for justice, protecting the water, people, and creatures who have suffered from our exploitation and violence. We can heed God's call to abundant life, to abundant water, as a gift of love for each of us.

Discussion Questions

- What are some local water-justice issues in your own community or city?
- How can we as a community of faith participate in lessening water consumption and decreasing the pollution of our local waters?
- How can we join in social actions that pressure our government leaders to stop damaging our waterways and polluting our natural water resources through drilling and fossil-fuel transport?

2

Intersecting Injustices

Environmental well-being is part of a broad network of justice concerns influencing and being influenced by how people relate to one another along identity lines like race, gender, class, nationality, and religion. When we live from our baptismal waters, we must recognize the many different ways that our community is shaped by intersecting realities within and beyond the church. Baptism does not erase our diversity; it enlivens it in holy love.

Injustice among people is never isolated to a particular kind of person, even if one aspect of a person is emphasized in his or her oppression. Racism is never contained only in race. Sexism is never contained only in sexual differences. Classism is never contained only in economic class status. We cannot talk about one without talking about the others, and we cannot struggle for justice against one oppression without struggling against all oppression.

Confronting ecological disasters means that we must address the intersecting oppressions that are intensified and created by climate change. We must address economic injustice, because climate change affects those who live in poverty, who are far more vulnerable to wage loss, food insecurity, natural-disaster damage, and more. We must address gender injustice, because women and children are more likely to be both impoverished and subject to violence from neglect, deprivation, and patriarchal culture. We must address racial injustice, because communities that have been racially marginalized are most often the communities where ecologically degrading industries like petroleum refining and chemical-waste dumping are sited. We must address at least these intersecting oppressions, for we live in an interconnected world. No single creature, no single identity, and no single location is entirely isolated from the rest of creation. As the waters of baptism teach us, we are knit together in a sacred body, hurting when one hurts and healing all together.

Economic Injustice

Climate change is a multifaceted present-day crisis with an enormous economic impact. Climate change, like many other ecological disasters, disproportionately affects the world's poorest people and displaces the most vulnerable communities. Those who are financially secure often have the means to find alternate shelter and move away from potentially harmful storms or climate catastrophes. The poor often do not have access to these means and must live through the disaster. So, even though climate change does affect everyone, its impact on the poor is seismic.

When Leonardo Boff teaches us "to connect the cry of the oppressed with the cry of the earth," he is calling us to tackle economic injustice as a vital piece of our struggle for everyone to live with clean water, clean air, and clean soil. He writes: "The logic that exploits classes and subjects peoples to the interests of a few rich and powerful countries is the same as the logic that devastates the earth and plunders its wealth, showing no solidarity with the rest of humankind and future generations."[1] The intimate relationship between climate and economic justice means that our struggle recognizes the connections between life itself and the quality of life that we live.

Environmental justice is about food, work, and human flourishing. Land that gives food and livelihoods to the most vulnerable among us is commodified and targeted for profit. Those who rely on the land for their daily food and to help produce income by selling their farmed vegetables or livestock can have their lives turned upside down in an instant. One strong storm can devastate a subsistence farm or a small community farm. In the storm's aftermath developers and land speculators can swoop in to exploit the financial and food insecurities of the poor. The poor may be forced to move or live in areas that have not yet been devastated by climate change. The same behaviors that exploit other humans for profit threaten and degrade the earth as a whole. Until we live in solidarity with the poor and protect the earth, this will only get worse. The rich will get richer by extracting all they can from the rest of us, including our planetary home.

Land and Sea

The land is one intersection of environmental justice and economic justice. Human communities have had economic

---

[1] Leonardo Boff, *Cry of the Earth, Cry of the Poor* (Maryknoll, NY: Orbis Books, 1997), xi.

relationships with the land for centuries, and we have had more holistic relationships with the land since time immemorial. The climate changes we are experiencing affect the land, those who work it, and what the land produces in those working relationships. For many—farmers, loggers, ranchers, and others—the land is their source of livelihood. As the climate changes, these people see their crops wiped out or so expensive to maintain that they become cost prohibitive, including feed crops for their livestock.

From the land we receive countless gifts, which we use for everything from fuel to building materials, from parts for our electronics to supplements for our health. Our extractive and financial economies distance us from the land and its gifts. In our current systems people who work the land or live close to the land are exploited as part of the land-based commodity structure. From coal to valuable metals like gold or cobalt, wealthy corporations are designed to plunder the earth of its gifts while keeping costs low. The costs to human and environmental well-being, however, are not factored into their financial calculus, and death-dealing atrocities are the result.

On farms, vibrant ecosystems that incorporate and support a tremendous diversity of life, including farmers and their family, are declared "not efficient enough" for the greed of agribusiness. Instead of small areas that are carefully tended to support many different kinds of plants and animals, each flourishing at different times of the year, large swaths of land are set aside to grow only one crop at a time. This practice is called monoculture, and it completely ignores how our planet has provided for us and been in relationship with us over millions of years.

One single crop can devastate the soil health over time, so fossil-fuel-based fertilizers are required to artificially support a growing crop. In addition to runoff from other agribusiness practices, these fertilizers leach into water supplies and eventually flow through our planet's rivers and into our ocean.

The land and the sea are more intertwined than our economic structures want us to know. Everyone will be affected economically by the devastations of climate change on our land and sea because every ecosystem is somehow related to all the others. The runoff from farmlands, lawns, industrial areas, and travel corridors eventually makes its way into our ocean, creating huge "dead zones" where little if any life can survive. The poor often live in the places where land and water meet, on rivers and seashores, because of historic abundance in the seas and fertility on the land in these places. Without the gifts that our land and sea provide, they suffer more and potentially lose their lives when dead zones trickle down from corporations that prioritize financial wealth over and against environmental well-being.

The pipelines that I talked about in the last chapter are often aimed at these fragile meeting areas of land and sea because the oil and gas that run through them need to be refined into products like gasoline, plastic, and lubricants before they can be useful to humans. That refining process requires massive amounts of water. As the Water Protectors from Standing Rock teach, every pipeline is a threat to water, and that threat increases at the end of the pipeline, where spills and leaks can be ignored as long as they are small enough not to disrupt refinement. The poor who live in these areas, held there by generations of relationship to the land and sea, have been invaded by the fossil-fuel industry, and they disproportionately bear the harms of environmental degradation.[2]

Wages

It is often the world's poorest who most acutely experience the cascading effects of natural and human-induced disaster. Many of the poor depend on agriculture for their livelihood. Whether they are small farmers, farmhands who sow and harvest, or those who transport produce to market, these are low-income jobs. Impactful events from climate change, such as extreme drought or storms, can wipe away their income for months or years.

Beyond the farms we see a ripple effect to the grocery stores that employ people to stock and sell food. Restaurants employ workers to prepare and serve food. If the farms cannot produce enough, or if the corporations that control the agribusiness intentionally limit supply, prices soar to take advantage of people's need to buy food to survive. If people choose to spend less time shopping or to dine out less often than they used to, companies can decide that fewer employees are needed. Cutting costs by cutting jobs affects both employees' wages—or lost wages—and the places that employees would patronize if they had income to spend. It's a horrible cycle that eventually extracts from and exploits everyone who is not rich enough to escape it.

---

[2] Antonia Juhasz, *"We're Dying Here": The Fight for Life in a Louisiana Fossil Fuel Sacrifice Zone* (New York: Human Rights Watch, 2024).

Resource Insecurity

As the temperature continues to rise and break records globally, climate change is affecting water supply, food distribution, health, living standards, and accommodations. The impact of climate change is greater in the areas that are already struggling, such as the Pacific Islands and many parts of Asia and Africa. Already some islands in Asia are slowly disappearing as the sea level rises due to the warm temperatures and the melting of icebergs. Rising seas will result in climate refugees, damage to traditional cultures, and increasingly frequent and severe floods where land meets sea.

Our current economic structure values the accumulation and protection of wealth to such a degree that millionaires and billionaires hoard vast amounts of money, land, and property. Hoarding intentionally limits the possibility that other people can meaningfully access the necessities of life with dignity. As I mentioned earlier, hunger is a policy choice. Food insecurity—the inability for people in impoverished areas, from inner cities to isolated rural locations, to get fresh, quality food that is nourishing and sustaining—is a choice that is made against the poor by corporations and governments that determine people's value by how much money they have or can produce. The waters of baptism teach us that a person's value is found in that person's creation in the *imago Dei,* the image of God, and the lifegiving relationships of love that fill our world.

Hoarding also produces climate refugees. When climate change devastates an area, either through natural disasters—floods, tornadoes, and droughts—or through pollution and industrial degradation, residents are inevitably displaced. When people are prevented from living with dignity so that the rich can stay rich, entire communities are left financially unstable. In the wake of disaster they are often left unhoused or must relocate to new areas where they have no support system, may not have options for employment, and, having lost most or all of their possessions, must start over.

Decisive action to address climate change must prioritize economic justice. Poor communities and people are at the greatest risk, have contributed the least to the current crisis, and provide the labor for the wealthy to have and hoard whatever they can buy. "How can the economy be doing well if Earth is doing poorly?" Boff asks.[3] Our decisive action at the intersection of ecological and economic justice must focus on the sustainable well-being of Earth for all humanity, creatures, and environments.

Greed and Overconsumption

Through the priorities of capitalism, European and North American values have exported a colonizing and dehumanizing greed to nearly every culture on the planet. Many of us want to eat more than we need, have more money than we can ever spend, acquire more material than we can ever imagine, and hoard that money and material away from others. Gluttony and greed twist together to form a strong cord that selfishly prioritizes our wants over the common good. They significantly contribute to this climate crisis, driving consumption to increasingly wasteful levels for the rich while denying the poor any meaningful access to the material conditions that support a dignified life. We

---

[3] Boff, *Cry of the Earth, Cry of the Poor*, 134.

are destroying Earth as we strip it to meet insatiable desire and have no plan for replenishing it, let alone honoring its gifts.

Consumerism has become a new civic religion. Regardless of other faith or spiritualized commitments that we might have, many of us are purchasing more than we are ever capable of consuming in a lifetime. In our search for meaningful life, neoliberal capitalism has commodified most of life itself, and it teaches us to equate happiness with possessing and consuming commodities. But this is a false ideology, and we must recognize that producing, shopping for, buying, and consuming more stuff does not bring lasting joy or support abundant life. However, it does bring damage to our environment, to our common home.

This new religion thrives on debt and desire. That results in further dissatisfaction and unhappiness as people attempt to spend more to try to avoid indebtedness in the future or pay off indebtedness from the past. People give their time, money, and energy, joining the world in an economic ecumenism, becoming good-willing disciples by buying and hoarding.

Within the successful advertising and marketing campaigns of consumptive capitalism, we have been conditioned to want what our neighbors have—or better than what they have. They are no longer neighbors but become competition in a covetous race for approval from the wealthy, who exploit us at every turn. Believing that our deepest value comes from what we wear, use, and exploit, many of us became motivated to maintain appearances for the jealousy of others at a very young age. In a show of devotion to consumerism, many people work long hours to attain its rewards and exploit those who work just as long or longer without being able to afford the quality of life that consumptive capitalism promises. We go into deep debt to remain faithful members in good standing; we spend many hours a week shopping so that we might consume only the "right thing"; we sell ourselves through biodata tracking, social media usage, and exploitative advertising.

While we will not reverse the alienation and destruction of overconsumption and exploitative production without a multinational commitment to policy and cultural changes, doing so begins with one person choosing to buy one less thing, and then another, and then another. Because overconsumption and exploitative production depend on isolating us from one another and from our gift-giving world, we know how to break the hold that the religion of consuming has on us. We must live in true solidarity with one another, just as the waters of our baptism have taught us.

Religion and Economic Justice

Religious groups have always expressed an obligation to care for the poor. This is recognized as a moral imperative, and there are many efforts to offer assistance. For Christians, Jesus's instruction to his disciples is important today: "Truly I tell you, just as you did it to one of the least of these brothers and sisters of mine, you did it to me" (Mt 25:40). However, little consideration is given to the poor and the least in regard to the impacts of climate change.

Global economics, climate change, and social injustice issues all intertwine and intersect in ways that greatly affect us all; however, our siblings living in poverty are affected first and most deeply. The poor suffer disproportionately more from the results of climate change than the rich do, yet climate degradation is largely caused by wealthy countries. Its harshest and most enduring effects weigh upon impoverished countries. In our struggle for ecological and economic justice, the Spirit of the Lord can guide us to bring good news to the poor, to proclaim release to the captive, to set the oppressed free, and to enact God's Jubilee Year of debt relief. When we work together toward sustainability and saving this planet, we help the poor and the oppressed.

Climate Refugees

One of the most significant ways that the poor suffer in this climate crisis is being forced to relocate because of ecological disasters. Climate refugees are people who must flee their homes and towns that are destroyed by ecological disasters, including extreme flooding, drought, famine, heat wave, and toxic environmental damage from industry. Often these extreme climate events contribute to political unrest and violence that further unsettles people and communities.

As the number of climate refugees increases, it becomes more difficult to appropriate enough resources to provide means of survival for the people. During the Syrian crisis, for example, droughts caused farmers to migrate into the cities as their livestock were dying and the vegetable crops were not growing. The massive surge of people into the cities, looking for jobs and economic means to survive with no assistance from the government, led to tremendous civil unrest and ultimately war. Many who fled Syria for neighboring countries and the wider diaspora were climate refugees.

When disaster hits, those who have the physical ability, financial means, and property resources to flee are often able to find a safe place to weather the storm before returning to their homes to rebuild. If the disaster is great enough, they can relocate and start again with significantly less disruption to their lives because of how their resources seem to buffer them from the worst of the worst. The poor do not have these resources. Swift relocation often comes at a devastating cost; people lose their homes, their livelihoods, their families, and their community relationships. While no nation is immune to the effects of climate change, the intersection of economic injustice with ecological injustice means that the uneven distribution of wealth in our world is weighted heavily against the world's poorest people and regions, weakening already weak economic, institutional, scientific, and technical opportunities to cope, adapt, and thrive.

Even within the United States, climate change and its ecological devastations have already uprooted many. Forced relocation is no longer viewed as a remote possibility but rather a looming certainty for those whose homes and communities are becoming uninhabitable. Just recently, wildfires raged in California, droughts endangered food crops in the West, ruinous floods engulfed towns from the Dakotas to Maryland, and violent hurricanes rendered miles of shoreline almost unlivable.

In the winter of 2021 Texas was hit by a winter storm that caused massive power blackouts and more than 100 deaths. Countless lives were upended by damaged homes, failed infrastructure, and health and financial difficulties. But for the privileged, the circumstances were different. Americans saw this firsthand in the spectacle of US Senator Ted Cruz and his family boarding a plane to Cancun to escape the power loss, water scarcity, and bitter cold in Texas after the terrible winter storm. The poor do not have the resources or the means to escape a storm but must endure the pain and suffering of the severe storms caused by climate change. Some poor people end up losing everything, including their lives, while the rich can escape, protect themselves, and rebuild their lives quite easily in a disaster's wake.

For decades many US Americans have evaded the most profound threats of climate change, despite the accumulating evidence of crisis in our own backyards. As more people seek to migrate to the seemingly fertile economic and ecological opportunities in the United States, often fleeing the worst effects of climate change and related political violence in their home countries, we must confront reality. The choices we make about where to live are manipulated and contoured by both the politics that minimize climate insecurity and the financial incentives that fund resistance to the natural processes of our world's ecosystems.

American policymakers have left our country unprepared for what is to come. We now face devastating moral decisions about which communities to protect and which to sacrifice. In an already fractured society our choices can relegate the poor to a nightmarish future that leaves them unequipped to survive, let alone flourish. The crisis will not wait for the worst environmental extremes to appear;

it is already here. We must work mightily to correct this injustice before it gets worse.[4]

The estimated cost of climate and weather disasters in the United States in 2022 was more than $165 billion, which is the third most costly year in recorded history. This enormous amount does not cover the lives lost, the impact on our healthcare system, and those who have been displaced. The financial costs of climate change will continue to rise, having a deep impact on the US economy, as it does on the worldwide economy.[5] The financial costs will pale in comparison to the human and creaturely costs of mass migration in response to ecological disasters.

Gender Injustice

The intersection of ecological injustice and gender injustice is significant and emerges from the economic injustices mentioned above. When we think about the questions of survival that are related to environmental well-being, we must ask who has to deal with the regular tasks and materials that keep us alive on a day-to-day basis. Often, the answer to this question is: women. No Christian theological reflection on climate injustices can be complete without theological reflection on gender injustices, because our flourishing as the body of Christ and the creaturely communion of God's world cannot happen if we deny the full humanity of women.

---

[4] Grace Ji-Sun Kim, "Our Climate Practices Must Change Post-Pandemic," *Faith and Leadership Newsletter,* May 4, 2021.

[5] Candace Vahlsing and Zach Liscow, "The Importance of Measuring the Fiscal and Economic Costs of Climate Change," The White House, March 14, 2023.

Patriarchy

Patriarchy is the societal and cultural system that believes that men are superior to women because they are stronger, smarter, and more valuable to the world than women. As a result, men are given more education, better life opportunities, and gain more wealth. Consequently, women become poorer, marginalized, and oppressed. Many women are abused by men and told what they can or cannot do, and patriarchal cultures facilitate this abuse by dehumanizing or infantilizing women. In some patriarchal cultures women's movements are limited, restricting them from buildings, organizations, and events on the basis of sexual difference. In the extreme, women are limited to the compounds of familial land.

In patriarchal societies men are rewarded for positioning themselves against women. When a man gains in life, the gain is framed as against a woman. Women are often relegated to household work or familial obligations that would be considered belittling and undignified if a man was found doing that same work. A man's power grows from his ability to ignore, deny, and suppress a woman's agency and power as a person.[6] Patriarchy works to lower a woman's sense of being and self-determination by diminishing her power to control her own actions and achievements in society. It is nearly impossible to uplift women in a patriarchal society, because it is designed to keep them subordinate, subjugated, and controlled.

Women dwell in the valley of the shadow of death in a patriarchal world, compelled and pushed by men to assume

---

[6] Simone de Beauvoir, *The Second Sex*, trans. and ed. H. M. Parshley (New York: Vintage Books, 1989), 78.

the role of the perpetually subordinate and subjugated other.[7] Othering women exacerbates sexual difference, denies genuine community, and benefits men who are in control and seek to stay in power. The power-over dynamic is demonstrated in various spheres of society, even when women are told that they are responsible for some of those very spheres, like child rearing and housekeeping. The goal of patriarchy's power-over structure is to push women to the margins of society, including in family, neighborhoods, and churches.

Feminist and ecofeminist thinkers have been analyzing, critiquing, and theorizing about the role and identity of women for decades. Simone de Beauvoir identified a vital difference within heterosexual relationships, writing, "She is for man a sexual partner, a reproducer, an erotic object— an Other" through whom he seeks himself.[8] As the other, women are to be dominated sexually, physically, and psychologically. The reduction of women in erotic objectification has led to the violation and assault of women around the globe. Women have been made into objects, sometimes for sex and sometimes not, in many different cultures and societies. As objects, women can be violated, abused, and sexually assaulted without any severe repercussions, and their labor, including their reproductive labor, can be exploited to enhance the power of men.

To make matters worse, religious traditions have encouraged and can encourage the oppression of women in both teachings and practices. In certain cases, such as in Christianity, some denominations believe that this hierarchy of

---

[7] De Beauvoir, xxxi, xxxv.
[8] De Beauvoir, 59.

gender is not a cultural aspect but an actual direct commandment from God. This view argues that God ordained patriarchy and created some human beings to dominate and others to be dominated. Patriarchy, however, is evil and destructive, breaking women's bodies, minds, and health.

Gender and Climate Injustice

As we consider the climate injustice occurring in all parts of the planet, we recognize that some are more affected by this climate crisis than others. We know that climate change will result in a worldwide humanitarian disaster. We have already explored how climate change affects the poor more than the rich. We must also understand that climate change affects women in different ways from men. When extreme weather devastates a community, the inequality for women worsens as intimate-partner violence increases, girls are pulled from school, daughters are married early, and women and girls are forced from their homes and face a higher risk of sexual exploitation and trafficking.[9]

When we consider the Global South, girls and women bear an unequal responsibility for the performance of daily household tasks. They need to secure food, water, and other resources, as well as care for the young and the old. The processes by which women gather fuel for cooking, and the distances that women need to travel to collect water for drinking, cooking, and cleaning, have been greatly complicated by changing climates. In their experiences of day-to-day survival, we can witness the intersections of

---

[9] "How the Climate Crisis Fuels Gender Inequality," *CNN Special Report*, November 30, 2023.

ecological, economic, and gender justice concerns.[10] In societies, wealthy and poor, where women's roles in the home and family are particularly expected, women have less mobility in the face of severe weather, flooding, drought, famine, and political violence. Geographically binding family obligations seem to be thrust onto women, while men are either alleviated of the responsibility or sent abroad to labor as a climate migrant in a foreign land. Economic and ecological exploitation breaks relational bonds by reinforcing patriarchal stereotypes about women and men alike.

In the event that a woman is expected to be the sole economic provider for herself or a family, the economic gender gap presents more challenges for earning an education, entering the labor force, earning a living, and participating in decision-making and policy-making arenas in the world.[11] If a woman loses her husband, male partner, or other significant family connections, she is even more compromised. Girls and women also face gender violence, harassment, assault, and sexual abuse at prolific and disproportionate rates, which compromise their access to support for daily living. Hope dwindles, and their physical, mental, and spiritual well-being is lost. The welfare of young girls and women needs to be a priority, but in patriarchal societies they are at the bottom of the hierarchy and suffer tremendously for it.

In the wake of ecological disasters that render shelter, subsistence agriculture, and medical care impossible or unfeasible, families have been separated by circumstance,

---

[10] Gabriela Carbo Zack, "Five Facts about Gender Equality and Climate Change," United Nations Foundation, March 16, 2022.

[11] World Economic Forum, *Global Gender Gap Report 2023* (Geneva: World Economic Forum, June 2023).

tragedy, and force. Typhoon Goni in the Philippines fractured families as rushing water and a volcanic mudflow tore loved ones from one another. Severe drought in Afghanistan forced a mother to make the excruciatingly tragic choice to sell her daughter to feed the rest of her family. When Hurricane Matthew hit Haiti, children who were separated from or lost their parents were preyed upon by human traffickers. As a means of coping with disasters from storms, child marriage in places like Bangladesh, Ethiopia, and Kenya has become a way to secure funds or assets and recover losses due to devastating storms.[12] The havoc of ecological degradation forces people to last resorts as a means of survival for women and their children.

Patriarchal priority for men in the labor force often means that poor men leave home when climate disasters occur. The absence of sons, fathers, brothers, and husbands breaks families and means that the consequences of climate change are usually more acute for poor women and children. With the complexities of racial identities and racism, racialized people, and especially racialized women, suffer more due to their lower economic status and lack of access to dignified means of survival. The economic consequences are dire, and the health consequences are deadly.

Injured or sickened amid severe ecological catastrophe, women face longstanding gender inequalities that have created disparities in information, mobility, decision making, and access to resources and training in healthcare settings. Women are not listened to, believed, or taken seriously in the healthcare of their bodies because their experiences of

---

[12] "New Report: Why Climate Change Impacts Women Differently than Men," *United Nations: Climate Change,* June 10, 2022.

life and the world are limited and discounted as less than true. As Ivone Gebara notes in her classic, *Longing for Running Water*, we must "recover our *human experience*—to permit the meaning of our deepest beliefs to develop in our minds and bodies."[13] When women are valued and active in recovering our human experience, we participate in "struggling against certain alienations that hold us captive to an authoritarian system that limits our ability to drink deeply of our own experience."[14] Within those authoritarian systems, women and girls are less able to access relief and assistance when calamity strikes, further threatening their livelihoods, well-being, and recovery, fostering vicious cycles of vulnerability to future disasters.[15]

Beyond the acute healthcare concerns of immediate disasters like storms, climate change also threatens women's long-term health in unique ways. Women's reproductive systems are affected as heat waves increase temperature, creating conditions for vector-borne diseases such as malaria and Zika virus. These can increase the risk of miscarriage, premature birth, and anemia among pregnant women. Prone to experience food insecurity at higher rates than boys and men, chronic diet-related conditions emerge and are intensified in extreme weather conditions.[16] The vulnerability and defenselessness of women is clear in many places around the planet.

---

[13] Ivone Gebara, *Longing for Running Water: Ecofeminsim and Liberation* (Minneapolis: Fortress Press, 1999), 50.

[14] Gebara, 50.

[15] "Explainer: How Gender Inequality and Climate Change Are Interconnected," *UN Women*, February 28, 2022.

[16] Carbo Zack, "Five Facts about Gender Equality and Climate Change."

As women suffer more due to climate change, we must work to protect both them and their children. To undo some of these injustices we must dismantle patriarchal culture within and beyond religious traditions, including Christianity. The work of gender justice and climate justice intersect at many points: survival, health, physical security, economy, dignity, and relationships. In certain areas of the world women bear a disproportionate responsibility for securing food, water, and fuel; farming is the most important employment sector for women in low-income and lower-middle-income countries. During periods of drought and erratic rainfall, women, as agricultural workers and primary procurers, work harder to secure income, food, and resources for their families. This puts pressure on girls, who often leave school to help their mothers manage the increased burden. This decision cascades, affecting their future, as girls who are less educated are more likely to live poorer lives. Climate change escalates the social, political, and economic tensions in fragile and conflict-affected settings. These settings include the sexual differences between men and women and the gender imbalances enforced by patriarchy's exploitations.[17]

Environmental Racism

There has been a long history of noxious and hazardous facilities being located within or close to racialized minorities and low-income communities. While racial minority groups were involved in environmental activism prior to

---

[17] "Explainer: How Gender Inequality and Climate Change Are Interconnected."

the twenty-first century, a sustained movement that is focused on environmental inequalities has arisen within these communities in the last three decades.[18] "Environmental racism refers to any policy, practice, or directive that differentially affects or disadvantages (whether intended or unintended) individuals, groups, or communities based on race or color," Robert D. Bullard notes. "Environmental racism combines with public policies and industry practices to provide benefits for whites while shifting industry costs to people of color."[19] As I discussed in the context of water justice and baptism, Christian work for ecological justice must continue to expose how pollution is dumped into poorer, racialized neighborhoods; how this affects their health, life span, and quality of life; and how we can contribute to the struggle for justice.

Flint, Michigan

Water distribution in the United States and the quality of the water often correspond to the income levels and racial identities of an area. For example, in Flint, Michigan, the drinking water became contaminated with toxic levels of lead and other heavy metals as a result of municipal infrastructure choices. Flint changed its municipal water supply from Lake Huron to water from the Flint River on April 25, 2014. This change caused distribution pipes to corrode and leach lead and other contaminants into

---

[18] Dorceta E. Taylor, *Toxic Communities: Environmental Racism, Industrial Pollution, and Residental Mobility* (New York: New York University Press, 2014), 1.

[19] Robert D. Bullard, *Dumping in Dixie: Race, Class, and Environmental Quality*, 3rd ed. (Boulder, CO: Westview Press, 2000), 98.

the municipal drinking water.[20] Lead pipes were not replaced when lead was determined to be a dangerous contaminant, and toxic water was distributed to residents for their daily needs. Residents fought for nearly ten years to restore their water to acceptable levels of safety. It was only after prolonged and widespread public outcry over the injustice around infrastructure decisions that the issue was addressed.

Flint's population is around 60 percent African American and around 34 percent white. Black communities are disproportionately affected by water-justice issues related to poor infrastructure, dumping, and industry runoff. The relationships between government and industry often mean that regulators do not tackle environmental racism concerns even if there are regulations to enforce. The municipal government was slow to rectify the problem of replacing lead pipes in this community of color, and the switch to a new water source for the town exacerbated their neglect.

Native Americans and Indigenous Peoples

Environmental racism includes how Native Americans and Indigenous Peoples around the planet are treated. From discounting spiritually holistic approaches to environmental well-being to genocide against them, the animals they hunt, and the plants they gather and cultivate, colonial and settler-colonial societies have actively destroyed Indigenous life in the name of profit under capitalism. The intersecting

---

[20] Centers for Disease Control and Prevention CASPAR [survey], "Story: Flint Water Crisis," CASPAR, April 8, 2024.

injustices against these peoples and Earth confront us with the profound consequences of the climate crisis.

Indigenous groups around the globe have long been calling on governments, religious groups, and communities to work together to stabilize the climate. They seek some justice for their abused land. Indigenous groups are the racialized communities most affected by climate change because legacies of genocide against them have often left them on the margins of society. Large corporations, governments, and small landholders alike have swindled, exploited, deprived, and killed Indigenous People and their lands from the United States to Australia, South Africa to Brazil, New Zealand to Canada. Decades and centuries of government policies reinforce Indigenous dependency and suppress self-determination so that corporations, governments, and non-natives can continue to rob and corrupt the land with industry, infrastructure, and impunity.

Indigenous Peoples have particular understandings of climate justice that are integral parts of their spiritual relationships with the environment. These lifeways have been widely ignored, trivialized, or misappropriated by the rest of the world. It has been their way of living for thousands of years and is part of their identity and culture. They have a lot to teach us as we seek ways to change our lifestyles for the future of this planet.

Their understanding of the sacredness of creation and life is something that non-Indigenous people cannot seem to comprehend. Indigenous people cannot divorce the present-day land from the land of their ancestors, as their ancestors' spirits roam the land with their peoples, conversing with them and guiding them. Indigenous Peoples remind us that the spirit exists within all things. The spirit reminds us that animal populations often embody a spiritual aspect, making their preservation as valuable as human lives. This spirit is understood in different ways in different cultures. Indigenous groups remind us of the interconnectedness of spirit and nature.

In Asian cultures this is called *Chi*. Asians also believe that *Chi* resides in all living things. It is the spirit of life—it is what gives life to all living things. When we recognize that the spirit dwells in all living things, we are motivated to respect and take care of God's creation. It should motivate us to not damage or waste what has been entrusted to us but to try to live sustainably to save the planet and all living things on the planet.

Dominant forms of Christianity rejected this spirit-filled approach and divided our lives between spirit and body, between spirit and the natural world. As Christians continue to perpetuate the idea that the body/nature is bad and the spirit is good, we can justify environmental racism by dismissing communities of color and their material needs for survival and telling them to just focus on a heavenly reward for their suffering. Without ever seeing the interconnectedness of the spirit and the body/nature, we can reinforce environmental racism's destructive treatment of real bodies and real ecosystems in our world. When we have neglected to see the spirit as part of the natural world, we neglect to experience the fullness of Christ's incarnation among us. In Jesus, God took on flesh, and that was good!

Animisms and shamanisms have been condemned as focused on the "bad" spirits that possessed people and caused bad things on the earth. This negative and disingenuous view of the spirit in creation continues to haunt our own ways of being today. It has led to disrespecting people who believe in different ways from white Eurocentric ways. The disconnection and even vilification of the spirituality of Earth has led us to fail in being good relatives with one another and to other creatures, protecting and caring for God's creation.

We have forgotten and denied that the Spirit of God the Creator resides in all of creation and that taking care of creation needs to be our top priority if we want life to continue on this planet. As Christians who struggle for ecological justice, we must incorporate this understanding and move away from the dualist separation of the body from the spirit. Moving away from dualism can help us connect land and spirit, which will motivate us to reevaluate the rules of our households to incorporate better regard and care for one another and all of creation. We do this in the hope of living together in a world less pained, in a world of greater peace. It reminds us that there needs to be equity, respect for the land, and a transformation of humanity by the Spirit. It reminds us that all life is precious and that all faith communities must stand in solidarity with Indigenous groups at the front lines of fighting climate change.

Indigenous people remind us that spirituality comes from the natural world—a place that encompasses all we need: water, land, air, and all that lives therein. We all are vulnerable at this time, but colonialism has made Indigenous Peoples the most vulnerable, and we need to stand in solidarity with them and fight for the planet's future. We cannot live oblivious to Indigenous Peoples' warnings, for they describe the impact of our actions on creation. We cannot turn away from the reality of vanishing species in mass extinction. We cannot ignore Earth's painful cries in mega-storms, severe droughts, rising sea levels, melting icebergs, increasing temperatures, and deadly forest fires. We must heed these warnings and move in a sustainability-conscious faith, respecting God's creation, uplifting oppressed peoples, and embracing the lifegiving Spirit that fills all of creation.

Creation must be saved. This planet is our only home, and all of us need to take concrete actions toward saving it. We must take swift and meaningful action in our advocacy, our theological engagement, and our policy-making and enforcement for any changes to occur in working toward saving the earth. From intersections of injustice, we can interweave justice and peace.

Discussion Questions

- How are women affected more by climate change than men? How can we work toward gender justice and solving this problem?
- Where is the intersection of climate justice and racial/cultural justice failing? What changes do we need to make to protect underserved communities of color and Indigenous Peoples?
- How are gender, racial, and economic injustices intertwined? How can we work toward a holistic justice so that we can also achieve climate justice?

3

Exploring Theology at the Intersection of Climate and Justice

In 2012, Pew Research Center completed an ambitious study of international religious life. It found that a shocking 84 percent of people around the world are attached to one religion or another.[1] These religious people include political leaders, scientists, professors, teachers, lawyers, engineers, writers, doctors, farmers, small-business owners, artists, stay-at-home parents, and family caregivers. Religion affects our daily decision-making processes and determines our ethical choices and ways of living whether we are particularly religious or not. Whether we are shopping for food, buying clothes, traveling, consuming resources, or seeking entertainment, we often make decisions that are influenced by religious commitments. Even in countries that have legally separated religious institutions from government institutions, legislation, policy enforcement, and societal interpretation of laws and customs are influenced

---

[1] The Pew Forum on Religion and Public Life, *The Global Religious Landscape: A Report on the Size and Distribution of the World's Major Religious Groups as of 2010* (Washington, DC: Pew Research Center, 2012), 9.

by how people feel about religion—their own and that of others—and that includes how people think God or other significant religious figures want them to behave.

Personally, you may be done with religion, but religion is not done with you. Tremendous shifts have been occurring in the human religious landscape since that 2012 publication from Pew. These changes and commitments are becoming more and more evident in how we view climate change and sustainability.

Religion intersects with the identity markers we covered in Chapter 2 as well as scholarly and popular traditions in the sciences, politics, arts, and philosophy. Religious practice, instruction, and understanding—what some traditions might call faith—inspire us to act in particular ways and toward particular goals in our personal and communal lives. Religious life is a foundation for how we function as humans. Because of this influence, the world's religious traditions must understand their power in all aspects of our society and direct their adherents to move toward responsible behavior, especially in our environmental relationships.

Religious community is our best source of support for addressing the climate crisis. Through religious communities and relationships with those who are religiously committed, people can be energized to grow in ways that fulfill a hunger for social justice, including climate justice. This is one issue on which Christians can unite. No issue so grievously violates the core of Christian convictions as jeopardizing human life and God's creation through human-induced climate change. Our work for justice and peace in the world plainly puts us at the intersections of climate, economic, gender, medical, food, water, migration, and racial justice. Together, we have an opportunity to create spiritualities that participate in the Spirit's lifegiving empowerment of human and creaturely flourishing.[2]

As we creatively and lovingly take this opportunity, we need to reexamine religions, including our own Christian tradition, to see how we can interpret scriptures and practice God's commands so that we create a new world, with God, where all of creation can thrive. We need a liberative scriptural hermeneutics, moving us away from oppressive, dominating, and deadly readings of scripture and into freedom for life abundant. We need to engage religious teachings, reinterpreting some, abandoning others, and doing the reflective work for our own times and contexts to embody God's liberative love. As we seek to follow God's life of flourishing, creation, love, and growth, we can pray, sing, think, act, and live in the beautiful diversity of our world.

The world's religions must work together for the betterment of our planet. In some traditions interreligious or multi-religious work is discouraged because of beliefs about exclusive access to religious truth. The well-being of our many different environments, other creatures, and our human communities cannot happen if we prioritize these supremacist views. Our differences are sources for beautiful contrast not destructive conflict, so we must remake our societies together and restore Earth's flourishing health. If we do not work together, instead fighting tooth and nail, we will end up destroying our chances at abundant life on Earth.

Many religious organizations and faith communities are taking heed of this ethical and existential challenge and

---

[2] Diarmuid O'Murchu, *Ecological Spirituality* (Maryknoll, NY: Orbis Books, 2024), 184.

are making climate change a priority, understanding that we cannot continue to ignore the topic of climate change while all of God's creation is suffering. We must be able to continue to fight for the freedom of all people from environmental injustice. We need to give climate change the high priority it demands. In the Christian tradition, the World Council of Churches is taking a lead in this regard and hopes to inspire all churches and faith communities to do likewise. We can come together in the solidarity of climate justice work. A better world is possible, and religious people have a crucial role to play for that world.

Christian Misinterpretations, Misbehaviors, and Mistakes

I am a Christian theologian, so I feel particularly responsible to help Christians view and act in the world with love and grace. Regardless of their connection to Christianity, Christianity and the Bible have had a big impact on how people act in, behave toward, and view the world. Thus, we must be honest that a part of how we got into this climate crisis is due to our own Christian faith, belief systems, and interpretations of scripture. Our misinterpretations, misbehaviors, and mistakes have contributed to the climate change we are facing today.

Christians tend to view ourselves as the highest form of God's creation, and that arrogance has negative consequences. Many Christians believe that as the last created in the biblical creation stories, we humans therefore must be the pinnacle of creation. Furthermore, we human beings are created in the image of God, and this commitment has been interpreted to mean that we are the best of creation, for we are like God. We have read verses of scripture—verses like "God blessed them, and God said to them, 'Be fruitful and multiply, and fill the earth and subdue it; and have dominion over the fish of the sea and over the birds of the air and over every living thing that moves upon the earth'" (Gn 1:28)—as justification for any behavior we see fit in our relationship with other creatures and the earth. In this elevated role human beings have dominated and ruled the earth, serving our own selfish and greedy habits and lifestyles, creating havoc on the planet.

From our misinterpretation we have mistakenly spread this belief and ideology that we are the best of God's creation. We have set humanity over the entirety of creation, reasoning from a sense of species entitlement. Yet, when we take the experiences of ecological devastation from climate change seriously, we see that elevating humanity has been detrimental to the planet and to ourselves. Bad theology has resulted from our misinterpretations, misbehaviors, and mistakes. Because of different dominant strands of Christianity, humanity believes that we can take everything we want for our own use with little regard for the consequences of our actions on the well-being of others. We have gone beyond relationships with other creatures and the earth that cherish what is provided for us as gifts of grace. We thirst for more and more things that aren't necessary for our flourishing. We have gone to the point of violent exploitation of the earth to satisfy our own selfish desires for greater financial wealth and material attainment. We cannot continue to view ourselves as being valued over everything else. Christians cannot survive if we continue this road of greed and destruction, and we certainly can no longer pretend that our greed and destruction are faithful and Christlike behaviors.

The Christian conviction that God is the creator of all things can help us recognize and turn away from our misinterpretations, misbehaviors, and mistakes. There are theologians who can help us become more faithful Christians in solidarity for climate justice by tuning us in to God's creative love for the world. Some of them help us reinterpret scripture. Others help us behave in more Christlike ways at the intersections of justice concerns. When we read scripture carefully, we see there is no special day that is designated just for the creation of human beings. We were created on the same day as a lot of other animals. We all share the same biosphere, and, in our current ecological crises, these theologians can help us emphasize humanity's goodness as a creature. As bearers of God's image in the world, humans have been given a special task as caretakers of Earth. We do not come first, for we are responsible to all who have been put in our care.

Christianity Must Reimagine a Better World

For Christians, the ecological crisis is a theological crisis. *Who are we as humans?* is a question about our relationships with one another, all of creation, and with our Creator. The Genesis creation stories are fertile sources for beginning to answer this question in the context of all of our relations. Theological reflections on the scriptures, church teaching about creation and humanity, and our experiences of God as a loving Creator are crucial sources for responding to our current crisis.

Sallie McFague, an ecofeminist theologian, suggests that we may need to see our planet as a house that we can care for rather than a place of endless resources from which we take for our own personal use and gratification. Pope Francis has talked about Earth as "our common home." The word *ecology* comes from the Greek word *oikos* (house/home), so ecology is the study of organisms in their homes.[3] Ecology studies every living thing and how it interacts with its surroundings and other life forms. If we can focus our attention on the earth as a home, we may learn to become better relatives in our home. The Christian move toward solidarity for climate justice is enhanced when we return to Earth as our home, living and working with other believers for planetary restoration and well-being.

To become good relatives in our planetary home after we've participated in its degradation, we must confess our sin and repent. *Metanoia* is the Greek word that is often translated as repenting of our ways and changing direction. We need the actual change of direction today as we work for the climate.

When we change our direction, we can follow and extend Jesus's instruction to "feed the poor and clothe the naked" to include victims of climate change. We can rethink the Christian faith, decentering humanity and prioritizing the flourishing of all of God's creation. This challenges us to reimagine the way we live with one another, promoting sustainability, love, and solidarity. We are also challenged to experience God in fresh ways that promote well-being for us all.

---

[3] Sallie McFague, *The Body of God: An Ecological Theology* (Minneapolis: Fortress Press, 1993), 56.

Faith Communities

Faith communities are one of the most important places where we can reimagine how to live together to promote sustainability, love, and solidarity for climate justice. These communities are places where our lives are already clearly influenced by our relationships. It is easy to experience how we influence and are influenced by others in communities where we share worship, meals, small-group study, and spiritual support. Here, we can start with small, intentional actions for environmental justice and experience how our life together as humans can contribute to the well-being of all creatures.

Churches and other faith-based communities are called to enact climate justice, especially for the benefit of the most vulnerable communities around the world. Some Christians fail to recognize the reality of climate change because of their views of the Bible. Others do not believe in climate change because of culturally conditioned skepticism and devaluation of the evidence of science. Yet others believe that it is not the role of faith communities to address climate change, believing that it is not religion's job to engage in "political issues."[4] The crisis is an urgent matter of life and death, and interpreting it as merely political theater is a dangerous mistake that refuses to recognize how communities are knit together throughout creation.

No single faith community can do it all. There are groups such as Religions for Peace that bring people of different faiths together to work to find solutions for how to live sustainably. Other organizations such as Sojourners,

---

[4] Grace Ji-Sun Kim, *Making Peace with the Earth* (Geneva: World Council of Churches Publications, 2016), xii.

350.org, and GreenFaith work on climate justice in various communities and political organizations. Within Christian denominations there are often denomination-wide organizations that promote creation care and climate justice in partnership with organizations that we've already talked about, like the WCC's Ecumenical Water Network.

Whether we are from Jewish traditions or not, shalom can be a valuable frame for understanding our work together for climate justice as a work of creative and meaningful peace. Shalom is both personal—emphasizing relationships—and structural—replacing systems where shalom has been broken. In shalom, old structures that have been devastated by violence are replaced with new structures that create and promote a vital and abiding peace. With God, we can make the old ways of living new, reshaping the world we know into the world God has intended.[5] In the shalom frame, part of creation care came in the form of a Sabbath year, which allowed the land to rest and grow what it would naturally produce on its own without planting. During the Sabbath year no one was to work the land. In normal years a person's land was divided into seven sections. Each year, one-seventh of the land was left unplanted so that it would rejuvenate and so the poor of the community could raise food for themselves. (Another provision for the poor was the command to leave the edges of the fields uncut so the poor could harvest something for themselves.) All of these injunctions were concerned about the well-being of the land; the poor; livestock and wild creatures; and the landowner.[6]

---

[5] Randy Woodley, *Shalom and the Community of Creation* (Grand Rapids, MI: Eerdmans, 2012), 10.

[6] Woodley, 29.

This kind of a peaceable justice practice seems extreme when we have forgotten how to faithfully practice Sabbath in our own lives. Faith communities that are reimagined for climate justice can powerfully support Sabbath practice as a relational journey in the Spirit. Importantly, framing our work with shalom and practicing environmental well-being in local faith communities means that even people who are skeptical of the scientific proofs of climate change are welcomed on the journey for the earth's protection and sustainability in peace. We must all continuously provide imaginative possibilities for how the church, faith communities, individuals, and the academy can move forward to help save God's creation.[7]

Faith community is a Christian way to think about the relationships that we find meaningful in our religious life. As we practice our faith together in new and fresh ways, we are called to hospitality and learning beyond our Christian spheres. Religious people all over the world must recognize the value of our relationships and unify our collective influence in the struggle for environmental justice and positive change at local, national, and international levels. We cannot continue to ignore climate change while God's creation is suffering. We must act and invest in fighting climate change as it may be the only investment that will have direct results for a brighter and safer future. We need to invest in clean, renewable energy; reduce the global carbon footprint; reduce waste; and recycle and reuse more actively. As people of faith we need to take seriously our theological engagement, advocacy, and social action to avoid a climate catastrophe.[8]

---

[7] Kim, *Making Peace with the Earth*, xiii–xiv.
[8] Grace Ji-Sun Kim, "Women Rise Up," *RSN*, December 21, 2017.

Love Our Neighbors

As Christians, if we are to respond faithfully to Jesus's command in Matthew 25:35—"For I was hungry and you gave me something to eat, I was thirsty and you gave me something to drink, I was a stranger and you invited me in"—then we must take climate change seriously. The poor, who are the least of our siblings, live with grave risks, and we must be in solidarity with everyone to make a difference in people's lives. Earlier, we covered the intersection of ecological and economic injustice. Theologically, Jesus's command in Matthew moves us beyond theory and into action. When we reimagine the world as Christians, Jesus expects us to act for that better world.

Practically, there are many things that we can do as Christian communities and persons to help save the earth. We must invest our time and finances in ways that protect the earth and support sustainable development.[9] We need to move away from fossil-fuel use. We need to become creative with our buildings. We must use renewable energy sources for power, and we can re-purpose spaces to be community hubs throughout the week instead of sitting empty for most of the time. These hubs can have clear connections to climate justice work like gardens, composting, and environmental education and action centers. We must become climate conscious in our local communities so we can live safely and keep one another safe. As we become aware of our contributions to the climate crisis, we can become faithful Christians who fight the crisis by creating the world with God in peace.

---

[9] Grace Ji-Sun Kim, "Investing in Our Children's Future: Divestment, Sustainability, and Climate Justice," *Huffington Post,* October 1, 2014.

Stewards of the Earth

For many Christians stewardship has become more about giving our money to the church than about caring for God's creation or tending to our relationships beyond financial bottom lines. As we approach the different intersections with environmental justice, we must understand how we have misunderstood many parts of the Bible, such as Genesis 1:28, discussed above. And despite Mary's testimony that God scatters the proud, brings down the powerful, and sends the rich away empty, domination has been a large theme in and goal for Christian institutions and political systems. For much of our history, Christian theology has been used to support people who try to take control of the earth, animals, and other people, including those who have not yet heard the gospel and those who are not useful to the reign of the powerful. Even the vision of the human as a steward of creation has been twisted and contorted to fit paradigms of capitalism, commodification, and inequitable wealth distribution in the United Kingdom and the United States over the last two hundred years. As we reimagine a better world, we must also reimagine a better stewardship.

The creation stories in Genesis do more than tell us about how things "used to be" in our faith history. They orient us to how creation and all of our relationships as creatures are supposed to be, encouraging us to tend to the well-being of all creatures because of God's view of creation. "God saw everything that he had made, and indeed, it was very good" (Gn 1:31a). God's first observation of creation was that it is good and beautiful. Native American eco-theologian Randy Woodley intensifies this point, writing, "We see that God created everything, and everything that God created is described in Hebrew not just as good, but as 'really good!'"[10] God found joy in creation! Created in the image of God and called to rule creation, we must first look to the Creator to understand how to rule. When we pay attention to God, we learn to love the creatures who were created by a loving God, including our human neighbors and ourselves. Stewardship fails when we make it about resource management. We should look at creation and find joy in it, tending God's love for our whole world. Instead, we have taken it for granted and begun to destroy it.

As we consider our role as stewards of creation, we need to examine the relationship between the doctrines of creation and humanity. In Genesis 2:15, God put Adam in the Garden of Eden to till it and keep it. Our human relationship with creation is first shared through the soil. We are not better than creation. We are part of creation, called to co-exist and cohabitate on Earth as fellow creatures from the soil. Second, as tillers and keepers, we are called to tend to our relatives' well-being. In the context of consumptive capitalism, tending to our relatives' well-being means using only what we need to live with dignity and to share God's abundance in loving justice so that all have enough to live with dignity.

For too long the church's teachings about humanity have put human beings at the apex of creation. Some traditions, mostly in Orthodoxy, have interpreted that position with a priestly humility that brings all of creation to God through humanity and God to all of creation through humanity.

---

[10] Woodley, *Shalom and the Community of Creation*, 41.

Dominant traditions in the Latin West, especially through Reformed Protestantism, have interpreted the human as the apex of creation in the destructive ways that we have discussed already in this book. In the last five hundred years these traditions have emphasized both that humans are depraved in sin and that humans are uniquely favored among all of creation. We are the grand exception to the violence in the world, even if we are the cause of so much of the devastation.

A notion of the human as some exception to creation is the opposite of God's desires for our stewarding relationships within the earth. God calls us to move to save the earth, not destroy it. God calls us to love the earth as good stewards whose lives are bound up in the lives of all other earthlings. If we want to live into the image of God as stewards, then we must take care of all that God has created on this earth by cultivating a love for life that prioritizes the flourishing of animals, plants, and the whole environment. Christians have too often misread our role in Genesis, justifying exploitation and legitimizing greed as if they are divinely sanctioned behaviors. We have mistaken God's call to be loving tenders of Earth with being self-centered dominators of Earth.

The trajectory of our current relationships with the earth is catastrophic. We have let stewardship become about resource management, turning our creaturely relatives from beloved creatures of God into things to be used. We must recognize our culpability in the devastation. God's approach to stewardship is a moral priority for love and righteous relationships. In the story of Noah and the Flood, "the Lord saw that the wickedness of humans was great in the earth and that every inclination of the thoughts of their hearts was only evil continually" (Gn 6:5). Noah's story is an allegory for human relationships among one another and with the land. Humans had moved from tending love to spreading wickedness. This allegory may become all too real as climate changes lead to events not unlike Noah's great flood. God calls on us to care for the poor of the earth, living sustainably so that all people might have life and have it in its fullness. We must understand that the difficulties that we are creating are not only for ourselves but for all the animals, fishes, creatures, plants, and the entire planet. We must change our ways to make this earth a better place for all.

We need to heed and welcome the theological underpinnings of ecumenical efforts to be caretakers of creation. Making peace with the earth is not easy after we have caused so much destruction, but now is the time for leaders with insight into the value of creation left in our charge to make tempering climate change their priority. However, too often the riches of the earth are exploited and the lives of people who live in poverty are diminished with no thought given to stewardship or the gospel.

The Common Good

In *Laudato Si'*, Pope Francis reminds us that "climate is a common good, belonging to all and meant for all" (no. 23). Because it is for all, we are all called to the struggle for environmental well-being. As I mentioned earlier, we are not truly alone when we fight for the benefit of everyone on the planet. As we address the heart of the matter, we must face the complex cultural and theological issues that make space for and encourage the damages of climate change.

The gospel priority for flourishing indicts and convicts us when our theologies have been used to damage the earth and one another.[11]

The earth and its fullness belong to God, the psalmist writes (Ps 24). Living in right relationship with God, one another, and all of creation, we can find a beautiful and enlivening gift in the psalmist's words. We are not entitled to destroy the earth, to exploit its gifts and its people. God breathes life into each of us and calls us to share the earth with every other beloved creature. We actually get to share in and create the good life with each other, with God, and with all of God's creatures. That is the common good. Our struggle for environmental well-being is vital to the common good being a powerful force for life in our world.

Instead of a theological understanding of human exceptionalism, striving for the common good can help us read ourselves out from under biblical interpretations that have inspired and ordained our delusional faith in domination over the rest of creation. As a Christian value, the common good challenges all forms of supremacy, especially the supremacies of wealth, masculinity, and whiteness that we discussed in Chapter 2. We must approach our sacred texts and theological traditions with a fresh concern for the material well-being of all life on Earth. As we fight climate change, our theological imaginations must support community building for the common good as we read and engage the creation stories.

---

[11] Grace Ji-Sun Kim and Rev. Jesse Jackson, "What Matters to the Heart: Pope Francis, Climate Change, and Sustainability," *Huffington Post*, August 12, 2016.

Contextual Theology and Climate Justice

The word *context* comes from the Latin word *texere*, which means to weave or join together. When we are doing eco-theology, we are developing a contextual theology that speaks to the richly woven cultural, social, political, economic, and religious situation within which we live. Theology never occurs in a vacuum but always within a specific context, place, and situation. Thus, one needs to examine carefully the different historical, social, and political contexts within which we are developing our theology. The climate crisis sets the agenda for our theological context, creating an emergency situation with severe consequences for life on Earth.

All contextual theologies connect theology with social existence. Our social existence changes, changing theology within the limits of our own histories and places. Theological language is not, then, a universal language but a particular language for a very specific social setting.[12] Each group of people must develop its own particular theological language according to its distinct context. In addition to the contexts of biblical texts, the early church, and other eras of church history, our contemporary situations, cultures, and contexts influence our theological work today. We need to understand our present situation in order to be able to do theology well.

When I say that all theologies occur in specific contexts, I am challenging white European colonial theology to recognize that it is also responsible to and for specific

---

[12] James H. Cone, *God of the Oppressed* (New York: The Seabury Press, 1975), 39.

contexts, cultures, and places. In the theological academy in the United States, contextual theology has its social roots in the experiences of Christians who recognized that the theology they received was not an ahistorical, asocial, or acultural theology. It was also *contextual*, even if in an unconscious way. *Contextual theology* does not mean theology done by people who are not white or who care about non-Eurocentric communities. When done well and with self-reflection, theology tries to engage one's own culture, history, and concerns with integrity. One's context determines the kinds of theological questions raised and confronted by the theologian.[13] As contexts change, the questions also change. Sometimes, the changes are so significant that the questions and answers of the previous generation are not suitable for the next generation.

Douglas Hall outlines three reasons that theology is contextual. First, theology is contextual because it is a human enterprise. Human beings live and reflect in differing times and places, so we need to be aware of our contexts to speak adequately about God. Second, theology attempts to speak of a living God who relates to a dynamic creation. Critically reflecting on God will require us to also reflect on the signs of our dynamic times. Third, theology exists for the sake of the church's confession. Christians are called to communicate our faith and make it comprehensible for our own times and places.[14] Hall argues that "a theology which knows that it is not timeless will always need to know what time it is. Unless it knows this, the Christian

---

[13] Christopher J. L. Lind, "An Invitation to Canadian Theology," *Toronto Journal of Theology* 1 (1985): 17.

[14] Douglas Hall, *Thinking the Faith: Christian Theology in a North American Context* (Minneapolis: Fortress Press, 1991), 100, 107.

community will not know what form of the Word is appropriate."[15] Theology is appropriately contextual when it tries to provide hope as it speaks to its particular context and seeks to liberate those who suffer hardships, oppression, and domination within that context.

Within the context of our climate crisis, no one specific group of people can provide the questions or answers for all people. Our theological task is to encourage and learn from others as we critically reflect on God's gospel of abundant life in our own contexts, in our own ecosystems. We can imagine and enact a better world with one another and God, and that will require us to return to outdated modes of thinking and address their processes and results. This includes examining our images of God.

A Dominant White Male God

Our views and perceptions of who God is influence our thinking, beliefs, and actions in our homes, churches, and society. Implicitly or explicitly, Christian theologies have constructed images of God as a ruling-class male throughout much of our history. Today, images of God as a white male are used to legitimize unethical social structures, including patriarchy and white supremacy. Imagining God as a ruling-class man, Christian theologies have prioritized an omnipotent and unchanging God, emphasizing values of domination over and the destruction of enemies, including the earth, if God is made angry. In recent centuries white supremacy has so infected theology that "ruling-class male" theology has become synonymous with "white male" theology. This type of theological imagery about God only

---

[15] Hall, 81.

legitimizes our destructive behavior toward each other and all of creation.

The white male God exemplifies and intensifies the domination of white men through intersecting colonial, racist, and patriarchal oppressions in our world. The white male God is not a true image of God. It is an image of how white men and their supporters want to be seen: as God. This image is the platform for our violent desires to dominate the earth, people, and God's creation even if we are not white men. The white male God image lies to everyone, white men included, because it prioritizes behaviors and relationships that are not loving, flourishing, and creating life in and for our world.

We must create new theologies that prioritize environmental well-being as faithful to the scriptures and God's own life. As we do theology together, we must respond to our contextual realities and dreams by emphasizing the shalom relationships that we experience in the biblical creation narratives. Our theology will have to comprehend that being fashioned and commissioned in the image of God is not the same thing as being God. We are responsible for how we respond to God's calls and gifts in our lives, and our theology will have to talk about God in ways that are responsible to our contexts and to God's life alike.

Metaphors and God

Christianity has been using metaphors to talk about God from its inception, and theology will do the same as we struggle for environmental justice. In our theological shift to creation care, our language about God will incorporate different images and ways of communicating that support the love of life. Our understanding and reimagining of God should help us work toward liberation, change, and sustainability that secure environmental well-being.

Metaphors are figures of speech in which a word or phrase is applied to an object that it does not literally denote in order to imply a resemblance. It is a tool that expands our thinking, aiding us in comprehending intangible objects and mystical concepts such as God. Metaphors help give meaning and depth to another. In Christian theology metaphors are necessary tools to give our minds some way to try to imagine the incomprehensible. In many ways we cannot do without metaphors when we talk about God, because no one can understand the fullness and mystery of God. Since our experiences and conception of God are limited and imperfect, we resort to different tools to help our minds conceive of who God is. Metaphors have become necessary and important tools for us to make meaning in life and make sense of an infinite God who created all things. Metaphors help us comprehend by comparing something less familiar to something more familiar to us. A good and helpful metaphor can enable us to see and reimagine the world in a new light.[16] A positive and strong metaphor helps expand our understanding of complex thoughts and ideas. In theological discourse we use a lot of metaphors to help us get a deeper comprehension of who God is. For example, a common metaphor for God is father or king, and both can be found in the Bible. However, masculine and domineering images also do the opposite of helping us understand God more fully. Instead, these

---

[16] Grace Ji-Sun Kim and Susan Shaw, *Surviving God* (Minneapolis: Broadleaf Books, 2024), 45.

metaphors can break, destroying our images of God and reinforcing destructive relationships in our lives.

We must be aware of the limitations of using metaphors in our God-talk. Metaphors are products of particular cultures and contexts, limited by time and space. Metaphors can also function as a tool for those in power to maintain their power, keeping others subjugated and powerless. Metaphors are loaded with the preferences and biases of a culture. The metaphor of God as a king reinforces the political system of monarchy and has been used to legitimize colonialism and patriarchy as natural acts of the monarch. If God is understood as a king who demands our allegiance and faithfulness, an earthly king can demand the same from us under the guise of being divinely placed and supported. A step beyond monarchy, the metaphor of God as king can easily validate and reinforce colonialism. Colonizing kings can use their power to keep the colonized subjugated under their reign by instilling particular values of race or ethnicity-based subservience and obedience as God's own values. Seizing other people's land and resources, slaughtering them and/or erasing their cultures, languages, and identities then just become part of "following God's plan for the world."

Colonialism does not need monarchy. The United States emerged out of a colonial monarchy, Great Britain, and continued the colonial practices under a republican constitutional democracy. The king metaphor for God reinforced the images of empire and colonialism even in the so-called democracy because God became the new moral leader of the nation, spreading favor to settlers who could faithfully "civilize" and "moralize" a wild and pagan landscape. The

European settlers of North America and the citizens of the young United States carried on a centuries-long genocide against Native Americans in order to claim their land "in the name of God" and for the purpose of industry and civilization. White Christians claimed that they were destined by God to spread across the continent, explicitly connecting the settler colonial invasion of Indigenous lands to God's civility and morality. This was called Manifest Destiny, and it implicitly and explicitly developed the Roman Catholic Doctrine of Discovery.[17] Many settlers sincerely felt that they were doing the will of God by turning seemingly godless people into Christians. They placed Native American children in church-run and government-run boarding schools to be educated by white people so that their Native American cultures, languages, traditions, and spiritualities would be suppressed.

Theological metaphors are not innocent turns of phrase. They have material consequences in the world beyond any single setting or theological tradition. As we communicate our experiences of God's creating love and abundant life, we have a tremendous responsibility to care for our language about God. Our metaphors matter.

God Is Not a White Man

God as king is a metaphor that attempts to communicate divine majesty, power, and awe. It has also legitimized patriarchy and colonization in the name of God, advancing the church's evangelism or mission into the world in

---

[17] The Roman Catholic Doctrine of Discovery, developed in a series of papal documents in the fifteenth century, justified European conquest of non-Christian lands.

limited and dangerous ways.[18] Some of the mission work has been more about eliminating native practices, religions, customs, and culture as a way to civilize the new hearers of the gospel. Making them Christian came at the cost of their whole worlds.

The colonialism that dehumanized millions and destroyed the water, land, animals, and whole ecosystems of the colonized also emerged out of dominating patriarchal metaphors in Christian theology. The exclusive use of masculine descriptors like father and king for God has been prominent in Christian history and has reinforced the maleness of God. Furthermore, most of the church leaders and theologians in church history were powerful men. As whiteness became a social and political force in the 1400s and 1500s, these men wedded their patriarchal power to white images of God, reifying a white male God. Theological priorities for white patriarchy reinforced and legitimized the status of the rich and powerful. They still do. Our world could have been a different kind of world, where Christians do not oppress people, including other Christians, and where the image of God is not used to destroy creation and damage the earth. Metaphors help us understand complex ideas, but they also constrain our comprehension of them. They only portray a small portion of the complex idea. Metaphors such as king portray a male God, but God is not male and is not an old white man sitting up on a throne, high up in the sky. God is beyond maleness, for God is Spirit.

As we discussed the intersections of injustice in Chapter 2, it should have been clear that the problem of pa-

---

[18] Kim and Shaw, 45.

triarchal metaphors is influenced by and influences racial injustice and racist ideas. God as a king and other patriarchal metaphors are often intertwined with whiteness today. More than a mere priority for a particular race, whiteness is the ordering of society to value Eurocentric ideas, processes, and descendants at the expense of other groups of humans, other ways of living in the world, and other value systems. Analyzing the intersections of oppression, we can recognize how patriarchal metaphors overlap with whiteness to portray God as a white man to the detriment of people of color.

Emphasizing these metaphors, white male theologians and their students reinforced and participated in broader societal agendas, legitimizing the power of white men over women and people of color. Such an image worked for the white male powerful elite, but for all others it has been detrimental. God as white has deep consequences on people of color. If we believe God to be white, then we are predisposed to believe that white people are more like God than people of color. White European men lift God in their image and use the white male God to legitimize their domination over people of color around the globe. The white male God becomes the backbone of white supremacy, as how we imagine who God is affects our actions and outlooks in life. The white male God has legitimated the genocide of Native Americans, the enslavement of Africans, the indenturing of Asian Americans, and anti-immigration and discriminatory stances against people of color. God, who in our imaginations becomes associated with the most powerful white men, will continue to oppress people of color without new theological metaphors.

A quick look at our American society will show how white supremacy has driven xenophobia, Islamophobia, and other hatreds toward people of color. During the coronavirus pandemic the United States experienced an increase in hate crimes against Asian Americans, with murders and violent attacks throughout the country. The white male god supports white supremacy and white people's oppression of and discrimination against people of color. It upholds white people as the best and creates a hierarchy of people according to the color of their skin, with lighter skin at the top and darker-skinned people at the bottom. This delusional way of looking at different people, cultures, and ethnicities is distorting the creation story.

The images of God as a white man have legitimized racism and white supremacy. A white male image of God feeds Christian nationalism and white patriarchy within our society, contributing to discrimination, hatred, and violence against people of color and women.[19] This dominant Christian narrative and teaching has been with us for the last two thousand years. These are all evil systems, but Christianity and the church have normalized them and legitimized their evil actions toward people of color, especially women of color. Women of color have been dominated, sexualized, raped, and demoralized all in the name of Christianity.

Theological metaphors of God as a white man feed into dangerous narratives of domination, oppression, and suppression of people of color that also fuel the destruction of the earth. A white male God has led to the destruction of

---

[19] Kim and Shaw, 45, 46.

the earth, for it has allowed rich white men to do as they wish to gain more wealth to the detriment of the earth and their fellow creatures. It gives them god status and power to harm the environment to enrich their own pockets. To fight economic injustice, racial injustice, and climate injustice, we must seek alternative images of God that do not legitimize and reinforce these injustices in the church and our society. Rather we must seek liberative and empowering images of God that will motivate us to work for justice. In this time of climate crisis, we need to seek alternative images that go beyond the masculine metaphorical language about God. As we let go of notions of God as a monarch, we can open ourselves to God not as an individual actor but as the Source of all beings, the very Ground of being, the Beyond in our midst, a generative Ocean of Love, and a Creator Spirit who acts.[20] We get to go beyond the male and white metaphors of God and really embrace various other ways of talking about God.

Beyond a White Male God

Metaphors are just tools. They do not fully reveal who God is. God is beyond our limited imaginations, metaphors, and languages about God. As our contexts change, we need to be open to different perspectives, concepts, and understandings of God. We must not limit an infinite God to an old white man sitting up in the sky on a big throne, judging us and watching our every move. We must take steps to challenge, reimagine, and rethink God, putting

---

[20] Elizabeth A. Johnson, *Come, Have Breakfast: Meditations on God and the Earth* (Maryknoll, NY: Orbis Books, 2024), 19.

aside some of our traditional metaphors, languages, liturgies, and prayers, and be open to God's leading and the Spirit's leading in reimagining God beyond God as a noun.

Black liberation theologian James Cone articulated a theology of a Black Jesus, and this angered many white Christians. They felt offended and betrayed by such a proposition of a God who may be Black. God, who is Spirit, neither Black nor white, has been associated with white skin to such an extent that Cone's theological claim that Jesus was Black, a member of the oppressed of his day, seemed to go against centuries of church tradition. People question whether people of color are made in the image of God, creating images of God that resonate with their commitments to white supremacy. The strong manipulation of the *imago Dei* shows us the strong power in naming and describing the Divine. Naming God can reflect our human priorities more than our faithful discernment of God's revelation to us. God was created in the image and likeness of the white powerful men to serve those who are in power and leadership.[21]

Environmental racism emerges from these theological metaphors for a white male God. Damaging the health and economy of communities of color, this intersectional ecological devastation is undergirded by theological images of a God who, like the wealthy white industry owners, is too distant to care that pollutants are dumped into the poorer areas of a society, where people of color often reside and work. The continuous worship and praise of a white male God will only perpetuate environmental racism, for it will

---

[21] Wanda Deifelt, "And G*d Saw That It Was Good—*Imago Dei* and Its Challenge to Climate Justice," in *Planetary Solidarity*, ed. Grace Ji-Sun Kim and Hilda Koster (Minneapolis: Fortress Press, 2017), 122.

consistently and incorrectly equate the priorities of white capitalist men with the priorities of God.

The image of God as a white man need not be our dominant theological metaphor. It has enabled sexism and racism, intersecting with human exceptionalism and environmental devastation. New metaphors can enliven our Christian solidarity for ecological well-being and climate justice.

The Earth as God's Body

Some theologians have been helpful in explaining how we can combat our destructive lifestyles by viewing God differently from the patriarchal traditional views and understandings of God. Reimagining God away from patriarchy and whiteness can help us develop a stronger theological understanding of God, who encourages us to take care of the earth and not to destroy it or dominate over it. A theological perspective that motivates us to work for a sustainable and greener earth is desperately needed if we are to protect this planet.

Sallie McFague cares deeply about creation and all of God's universe. McFague argues that we need to reimagine God's creation as part of God's body. Reimaging the earth as part of God's body pushes our theological boundaries and our preconceived notions of who God is. McFague's proposition makes us rethink how we live, act, and move around in this world.

This way of thinking about God affects how we live day to day, for we would not want to hurt or destroy God's body. If God's creation is part of the body of God, our call to tender stewarding is a call to gentle, caring, and kind relationship with God's own life and body. Approaching God as embodied through our world can help us recognize the "God-ness" in all living things.

McFague points out that we are animals who cannot survive on our own. We need the other animals, plants, water, air, and Earth's other gracious gifts for flourishing. We are not islands unto ourselves. Within the body of God we are dependent on others, and they are dependent on us. Incarnate beings, we can understand the metaphor of our world as God's body, the enfleshing of interdependent relationships in our diverse and dynamic home. When we reimagine God and who we are in God, we can help change our course away from ecological disaster. As we reimagine the cosmos as God's body, we are lured to advocate for our planet and work for change. We recognize how we are partners in creation, stewards of love for the well-being of all.

Discussion Questions

- What images of God have you grown up with or have been using in your own life?
- What biblical images of God are present in the Old Testament and the New Testament that are more inclusive of all people and of women?
- How can we move away from a white male God to a God who welcomes all people and encourages us to do the same?

4

God Is a Verb

Chapter 3 challenged us to expand our understanding of and language about God as we respond to our current climate crisis. Our reflections on and thoughts about our experiences of God really have an impact on how each of us lives in our shared world. Traditional Christian metaphors about God do not seem to contribute to the flourishing of all creation. If we truly care about the well-being of God's creation, then we must explore ways of thinking and talking about God that can encourage us to live differently, striving toward flourishing and abundant life.

This chapter is about more than grammar. In our language to describe God, we must approach God as dynamic, relating to us and all the world with loving creativity. When we frame our experiences, reflections, and thoughts of God with verbs, we can recognize God as One who loves, creates, lives, forgives, thrives, beautifies, calls, empowers, enlivens, and the list goes on. Dynamically relating to all of creation, God the Verb can strengthen our own work to become loving creatures for the well-being of Earth. As we live, God lives with us, calling us to journey onward into environmental justice, abundant living, and healing love.

A Dynamic God

Sallie McFague, the ecofeminist theologian who helped us think about Earth as a household in Chapter 3, offers an intriguing metaphor for God and our relationship with God in our common home, our *oikos*. "We live and move and have our being *in* God. We might see ourselves and everything else as the living body of God," she writes.[1] Though we often think of a body as a noun, the living activity of all of creation challenges us to think of the body of God as dynamic. We can seek ways to live as better relatives within the body of God because we recognize that our lives contribute to God's inspiring and living presence. We are more than mere things on a stage. We are living in partnership with the earth and God to create, sustain, and celebrate life. Reimagining God in this way reframes our work toward environmental well-being as sacred work of loving justice.

Ecofeminist theologian Wanda Deifelt has explicitly argued that "the creative divine power would be better understood as a verb."[2] Read with McFague's insights, I think that Deifelt moves us in a helpful direction for talking about who God is at the intersection of climate and justice. Dominant ways of thinking theologically in Christian

---

[1] Sallie McFague, *The Body of God: An Ecological Theology* (Minneapolis: Fortress Press, 1993), 132.

[2] Wanda Deifelt, "And G*d Saw That It Was Good—*Imago Dei* and Its Challenge to Climate Justice," in *Planetary Solidarity,* Grace Ji-Sun Kim and Hilda Koster (Minneapolis: Fortress Press, 2017), 121.

history have used metaphors that rely on static nouns to talk about and describe who God is. Without the image of Earth as our household, even Sallie McFague's perception of the cosmos as God's body is a noun that can be limited to fixed and static visions of reality.

The static noun has reinforced that status is what really matters. As we discussed in the Chapter 3, white male theologies have twisted the Christian gospel to support and justify hierarchies of power. Christian theologies that emphasize male pronouns and metaphors are often calculated projections of patriarchal and androcentric assertions upon God that help powerful men maintain power structures that benefit them. Traditional masculine metaphors and ways of talking about God have led us down the wrong path toward climate change partly because they perpetuate societal hierarchies that privilege particular people based on their racial, gender, and economic status. This assertion of a patriarchal white God corroborates and justifies hierarchical power that allows and legitimizes acts of violence and power against others, including other creatures. As we recognize the enormous problems that occur under patriarchal white supremacy, we need new theologies that accurately proclaim that God is living with us to liberate the oppressed, especially the oppressed creation.

The change toward understanding God as a verb will help us move away from white, patriarchal, and dominating views of God that reinforce male domination, colonialism, and destruction of the planet, empowering instead flourishing and thriving for all. The use of male nouns about God is a religious monopoly of spiritual writings. This kind of power and domination reinforces social, cultural, and political realms that control women, women's bodies, and the earth. New theological metaphors that center verbs can affirm the humanity of women, who are also created in the image of God, by empowering women to embody and enflesh God and creative love in their own lives.[3] Enfleshing will help us to become aware of how other creatures' flesh is holy and beautiful in God's own life.

Most significant, dismantling the theological metaphors that rely on white masculine status reminds us that God is not some distant being. Rather, God is *being* itself, moving, acting, manifesting through the world, making God's presence known in the world. God is who God is. Thinking theologically with verbs can remind us that we cannot limit God's "god-ness" to stagnant metaphors and nouns. Scripture, church traditions, and our own experiences show the radiant movement, overwhelming goodness, love, and mercy of God through verbs that help us participate in holy loving mystery, for our thriving as earthlings. We must seek alternatives and reimagine God as a verb that radiates the being of God.

God Is "to Be"

Various theologians have used different images and metaphors to describe God. Thomas Aquinas used the image of a fire that ignites to show the presence of God in creation. Instead of seeing God speaking to make things happen, Thomas Aquinas believed that Love created the world as a verb. Instead of a finite essence, he talks about the *esse* of God. In Latin, *esse* is the verb meaning "to be." His theological focus on the importance of God's "to be" reframes God as action that cannot easily be put into im-

---

[3] Deifelt, 121.

ages. "To be" centers a mysterious God who is the origin of existence. The verb form comes from the dynamic sense of "be-ing," which is beyond a simple way of understanding existence to an inexplicable sense of existence.[4] Be-ing is active. God does not remain static but continues "to be." Focusing on God as be-ing brings a dynamic, ever-changing, non-static, moving God to our theological attention. Though we will never comprehend the fullness of God and God's ever-emerging activity, our theological speculations are important small steps for making sense of God and God's relationships with our world. Ever on the move, Be-ing God calls forth living and thriving throughout the creation.

We experience the holy mystery of God through overflowing life, which has no beginning and no end. **In a mysterious infinity, God to-be is creating the world and revealing life throughout creation by be-ing present among us.** Aquinas believed that God is within all things, not just as part of how all living things work, but as the actual be-ing of all things. God causes all things to be and preserves all beings. God is present and moves in all beings, and God's creative process continues even today.[5]

The divine mystery challenges us to reimagine God away from the traditional, patriarchal, and destructive metaphors about God that have reinforced colonialism, destruction, and climate crisis. More than unethical, these metaphors are inadequate because of how they limit an unlimited God. As we move away from those destructive metaphors, we can embrace this holistic and lifegiving theology of "to

---

[4] Elizabeth A. Johnson, *Come, Have Breakfast: Meditations on God and the Earth* (Maryknoll, NY: Orbis Books, 2024), 71.

[5] Thomas Aquinas, *Summa Theologica*, I, 45, 3.

be." Theologically, "to be" is liberating and empowering as it sets a dynamic, non-gendered, and non-racialized way of speaking about God. It embraces God's activity rather than status, transforming our ways of thinking about and relating to God for our lives today. More than a philosophical turn to Thomas Aquinas, this approach to theology appears in Exodus 3:14, when God speaks to Moses amid the community of creation, saying, "I am who I am."

From "to Be" to "I Am"

When a baby is born, the naming process is of utmost importance. For most parents-to-be, a list of names has been whittled down to a favorite over the months leading to the child's birth. Depending on one's culture, ethnicity, and practice, the honor of choosing the name might fall to an elder family member. In Korea, it is usually the paternal grandfather who names the child. Korean names traditionally carry the family's generational *dol-im*, which means one part of the three-syllable name is used by all the cousins born in the same generation. For example, in my husband's family, the *dol-im* is the syllable *Young,* and all his cousins have the same *Young* syllable in their names. Names identify your family and potentially define who you will become. If a child is given a name with a significant meaning, such as *Grace,* which means favor or blessing, the hope is that the being of that name will be conferred onto that child, and the child will grow up to be blessed or favored.

In the Bible naming was a sacred responsibility and held enormous significance. When God created the world, humans were given the task of naming the animals. The first quoted human sentence was an act of naming the woman.[6] The passage reads:

> Then the man said,
> > "This at last is bone of my bones
> > and flesh of my flesh;
> > this one shall be called Woman,
> > for out of Man this one was taken."
> > (Gn 2:23)

Power and authority come with the ability and honor to name. Names are who we are.

God's name is mysteriously unveiled in the Book of Exodus. When Moses encounters God, he asks what God's name is. God self-reveals to Moses as "I Am Who I Am" (Ex 3:14).[7] Notice the verb! *Am* becomes the identity of who God is. Instead of a who-done-it to be solved, the Divine Mystery is active be-ing in and through the world, calling us to participate in God's own living.

In biblical studies of the Hebrew language, this Exodus verse is significant because it reveals The Tetragrammaton, that is, the four letters that are the consonants of God's covenantal name. Connected with the stem h-w-h or h-y-h, "to be," the divine name provides deeper insight into the being of God. The form of the verb "to be" in Hebrew is imperfect or future tense, which could signify any verb

---

[6] Leon R. Kass, *Founding God's Nation: Reading Exodus* (New Haven, CT: Yale University Press, 2021), 21.

[7] Mark Semeth, *The Name: A History of the Dual-Gendered Hebrew Name for God* (Eugene, OR: Wipf and Stock, 2020), 22.

tense, past, present, or future.[8] This linguistic complexity enriches our experience of who God is as God is present with us today, in the past, and in the future.

Later, writers in Deuteronomy intensified this complexity, stating, "the Lord [YHWH] is God in heaven above and on earth below; there is no other" (Dt 4:39). This theological exclusivity could easily be used to justify empire-building, colonial destruction, and status-based power structures in society. God's conversation with Moses, however, helps us not repeat mistakes of Christian exclusivity and oppressive treatment of the religious other. When God tells Moses God's name, God also says that "the Egyptians shall know that I am the Lord [YHWH]. Even though, outside of Israel, a god with the name YHWH was not worshiped, God's be-ing could not be limited by a single kingdom, culture, or empire."[9] God's presence is not limited to our time and space, for God just *is*. God is beyond the limited scopes of our understanding.

The earlier version of YHWH, The Tetragrammaton, was a three-letter name, YHW. This name was pronounced "hu-hi" in the oral tradition, which is translated as "he-she" and was commonly understood in the Egyptian context as a way of talking of the pharaoh, whom they perceived as divine and embodying both genders.[10] This common dual-gender approach was probably also known by the Israelites under the Egyptian empire and can trouble

---

[8] George H. Van Kooten, *The Revelation of the Name YHWH to Moses: Perspectives from Judaism, the Pagan Graeco-Roman World, and Early Christianity* (Boston: Brill, 2006), 7.

[9] Van Kooten, 9.

[10] Semeth, *The Name*, 23.

heteronormative theological assumptions about gender and sexuality today. As we rethink and reframe our theology with verbs, God's own be-ing provokes us to challenge our societal and cultural views, too. Leon Kass has argued that YHWH means the One who orders the Israelites to build a sanctuary so God may dwell in their midst.[11] The name of God is understood to be in the active verb tense, requiring the Israelites themselves to act.

God's own self description has often been ignored in the Christian tradition in favor of metaphors to describe God that more easily display power and control. God's be-ing is difficult to conceptualize. It is hard to control and weaponize. As we dismantle the white patriarchal ways of talking about God that have been used to justify ecological devastation, God's own self-description in verbs is a significant turning point for us. Without hemming God in, we can understand our experiences of God through a liberating and exciting frame that also reorients us to one another and all of creation.

God's own way of naming Godself moves us away from relying on masculine nouns and pronouns that reinforce patriarchal structures that oppress women and the earth in our theologies and our world. God's own way of naming Godself moves us away from the whiteness that has painted God over the last few centuries and that has led to enduring legacies of racial injustice, especially environmental racism. People of color, women, other-than-human creatures, and the earth itself are crucified at the intersections of these oppressions. The Be-ing God

---

[11] Kass, *Founding God's Nation*, 22.

is not a death-dealing deity. Be-ing creates, lives, restores, heals, and loves.

God Is Creator

The idea of God as a verb offers a dynamic and productive reading of the story of creation, where we see God as the genesis of all relationships.[12] God is the giver of all by acting to create the world. God is not a passive God but an active God who engages in providing new life. God is the wellspring of goodness, as God creates the world and announces that it is good. In that first Genesis creation story the Spirit of God is hovering over the surface of the waters, "a spirit-rhythm as in the beating wings of a seabird, the oscillation of breath, or the ebb and flow of ocean."[13] In the creating, God moves with the emerging earth.

The Hebrew word for "create" is *bara*, which means "to bring into relationship." The author of Genesis used *bara* to denote God bringing forth into existence what had not been here before. Creation brings into relationship with the divine source of life. The phrase *God creates* means that God shares God's life with us.[14] God desires to be in a relationship with us and with all of God's creation. God doesn't create something and then abandon it. God engages with creation and wants creation to flourish, multiply, and grow.

---

[12] Deifelt, "And G*d Saw That It Was Good—*Imago Dei* and Its Challenge to Climate Justice," 131.

[13] Catherine Keller, *On the Mystery: Discerning Divinity in Process* (Minneapolis: Fortress Press, 2008), 49.

[14] Ilia Delio, *The Not-Yet God: Carl Jung, Teilhard de Chardin, and the Relational Whole* (Maryknoll, NY: Orbis Books, 2023), xv.

Creation exists because God exists, and God exists in creation. God and creation mutually co-inhere and exist together. The Divine is never alone, as God is a dimension of the whole.[15] If we pay attention, we can experience God in our midst throughout the world. We can actually witness how what we do against creation, we are doing against God. As we hurt or destroy creation, we are hurting God; when we destroy each other, we are destroying God, for God's presence is among all of creation.

Earlier we discussed how some readings of the first Genesis creation narrative have mistakenly justified human beliefs that we are the most important beings in all of creation. When we have acted as if we are the apex of divine creativity, we have been prone to very destructive practices in the name of human dominion over all of creation. Our climate crisis, along with the biodiversity crisis and other environmental catastrophes, is a terrifying consequence of these theological mistakes.

When we emphasize that God creates, we must also remind ourselves that we are part of the creation that God declares to be "very good" (Gn 1:31). Bringing us into relationship with God and every other creature, Creating God calls us into loving responsibility as tenders and caregivers of creation in our experiences of the "very good."[16] We are not lords over, above, or separate from other-than-human creatures and our shared world. We are kin.

All creatures are part of the beloved community of God's creation. We cannot talk about God without recognizing

---

[15] Delio, xvi.
[16] Deifelt, "And G*d Saw That It Was Good—*Imago Dei* and Its Challenge to Climate Justice," 132.

Earth, its inhabitants and living things, and the entire cosmos as part of the stories of our lives and histories with God. We are forever interconnected in the creativity of Be-ing and are called to take care of one another.[17] Being created in the image of God is a beautiful opportunity to act for the created world, for our thriving and flourishing. In gracious holiness we can become like God through the love of Christ and creating presence of the Spirit. We are in our world to demonstrate God's love, care, and goodness for the world. From the simplest to the grandest, our living embodies God who acts, who loves, who beautifies. God is not a passive God, and we are not called to static dullness, especially in the face of our intersectional environmental crisis. God acts, and we are to do likewise.

God is the inexhaustible Source of all being, the very Ground of Being, endlessly loving, and an astounding Creator Spirit. Be-ing God beyond our fullest comprehension, Creator Spirit empowers us to move and do what is right. Spirit inspires, birthing the world as a partner in creation.[18] We are part of this creation story and must take seriously our participation in it as we grow in our relationships with one another, creation, and God. We have a loving example of how these relationships support flourishing for all in Jesus's own life and teachings.

"I Am" Statements of Jesus

John's Gospel continues the phrase "I am" as God self-defines through Jesus. Jesus uses the phrase "I am" seven times. Jesus says, "I am the bread of life" (Jn 6:35), "I am

---

[17] Johnson, *Come, Have Breakfast*, 16.
[18] Johnson, 19.

the light of the world" (Jn 8:12), "I am the gate" (Jn 10:9), "I am the good shepherd" (Jn 10:11–14), "I am the resurrection and the life" (Jn 11:25), "I am the way, and the truth, and the life" (Jn 14:6) and "I am the vine" (Jn 15:1–5). The author of the Gospel uses these "I am" phrases to connect Jesus to God, foregrounding the Be-ing through whom abundant life is available now, and to show us how mutuality and interdependence bear fruit for the well-being of the world.[19] As Jesus moves, talks, heals, helps, teaches, performs miracles, and lives, the gospel writer wants to draw our attention to the flourishing abundance of Life that emerges through sacred relationships.

In our attempts to understand our experiences of God, Christians have often created Jesus in our image or, dangerously, in the image of whoever happened to be in cultural and social power at the time. We have used the resulting theologies to justify the devastation that we unleash on creation, people of color, women, children, and the poor. Through the incarnation God has become a human being—Jesus—and reveals and enfleshes deeper mysteries than any single body can exhaust or limit.

The "I am" statements are rich theological metaphors that do not rely on limiting God to a powerful male human body in order for us to relate well to the Divine Mystery and to creation. With the loving and lifegiving Christ, we must participate in the flourishing Life that is for all of creation. The "I am" of scripture, especially in John's Gospel, depends on the verb in order for the metaphor to work at all. Instead of recognizing the verb as a valuable theological

---

[19] Jaime Clark-Soles, *Reading John for Dear Life: A Spiritual Walk with the Fourth Gospel* (Louisville, KY: Westminster John Knox, 2016), 73, 102.

understanding, we have focused on the nouns that follow "I am." As we reimagine the theological wealth of the verb, we can live more fully into God's own self-awareness and life. We can stop valuing paternalistic control; we can breathe deeply from the holy mystery that God has no beginning or end, is Creator continuing to create. We can abandon the racist exaltation of a single group of humans as the definition of good, true, and beautiful; and love exceedingly in the sacred reality that God moves throughout the universe, making all things beautiful, amazing, good, wondrous, and true. We can repent for the ecological harms we've caused and supported, and advocate zealously for climate justice as a holy cause. When we change our theological focus to verbs, we can encounter Be-ing who is Loving.

A Loving God

A Loving God includes the dynamic movement, power, feelings, and action discussed above. "To love" is the verb in our theological shift. A lover, a noun, is someone who loves, mercifully and kindly creating opportunities for life's flourishing. Lovers cannot not act. To love is a holistic act with real-world consequences beyond some philosophical idea or emotional sentiment.

In his Letter to the Romans, Paul even goes so far as to say that God's loving is so holistic that nothing can separate us from God's love.

> For I am convinced that neither death, nor life, nor angels, nor rulers, nor things present, nor things to come, nor powers, nor height, nor depth, nor

anything else in all creation, will be able to separate us from the love of God in Christ Jesus our Lord. (Rom 8:38–39)

Despite what a greeting card might say, love is not merely a feeling or emotion. Love is enacting and revealing the mercy, kindness, patience, grace, and goodness that are pulsing as the heartbeat of the creation. God becomes God in the creativity of loving, and we are graced with the opportunity to live in God's creative goodness and mercy. God's way of love is a tender patience, showing us how we are to love God, others, and all of creation. McFague's metaphor of creation as the body of God can help us reorient our love for God through loving creation, and we can change our ways to live a better and more sustainable life for the whole earth.

Divine loving has always moved with and acted within our world. Love-in-Action could very well be another way for us to think about God in this framework of verbs. God engages with the people with an orienting preference for liberating the oppressed, feeding the hungry, clothing the naked, and freeing the slaves. Even if this shift feels radical to you, consider why you pray to God. We pray to God because we believe that God is acting in this world and acting within the world for good. The wind of God blows into the world to work within us to change the world for good. Indeed, we need the living, moving, breathing God to inspire us to act differently in the world.

We journey to see how the power of the Creator God is not raw "power over" but loving that "empowers with." God empowers us to love others, love creation, and love God back. God's creative activity and love bring into existence a world that changes and moves as it becomes a partner in its creation.[20] Loving creation continues to move the universe, continuously inspiring life as it participates in the activity of the Spirit in the world. The Spirit is the eternal power that transcends yet operates within all of creation, calling forth bonding, adventuring, loving, restoring, healing goodness. The Spirit shares divine life, goodness, and joy, birthing the universe and luring it into a completeness of unity. The unity of God can be realized only eschatologically, when the "kin-dom" of God is fully achieved. God's identity is in the future and, only at the end, do we come to understand fully God and God's movement within the world.[21]

God Is Jeong

In Korea we have a term of endearment and attachment: *jeong*. It is often translated as "sticky love." When a person sticks a hand in a jar of honey, it becomes so sticky that the fingers become inseparable. This is *jeong*—a sticky kind of love that does not let go. *Jeong* holds people together as the love becomes inseparable. This is the kind of loving that we experience in God, an active sticky love, pulling us together with God.

Jeong permeates the lives of Koreans, a source of joy and meaning to many people's lives. Difficult to translate into English, *jeong* is greater and more vast than what seems to pass as love in the United States; it incorporates affection, attachment, compassion, kindness, sharing, connection,

---

[20] Johnson, *Come, Have Breakfast*, 19.
[21] Delio, *The Not-Yet God*, 116.

and sympathy toward people and objects.[22] It is difficult to separate or untangle oneself from this sticky love. Even though you may argue or fight with your friend, spouse, or neighbor, *jeong* brings you back together. *Jeong* flows out of you to the other, causing you both to feel connectedness, affection, and love. There is no logical reason or validation for why one experiences *jeong*; it just happens, emphasizing how we need one another for survival, as we are social beings who require connection to thrive.[23]

Jeong resonates within one's heart and between individuals, similar to notions of collective emotion and community in many Asian and African cultures. The sense of collectiveness or community emerges as *jeong* diminishes the "I," blurring distinctions between persons that have become commonplace in individualistic and capitalist societies. Experiences of collectiveness, common in Asia, keep people accountable to one another. As a cultural emphasis, these experiences are largely absent in the Western world, and our theology has suffered because of this absence.

Reframing our God-talk with an emphasis on verbs and relationality, accepting and enacting *jeong* within Christian theology can be an important way to live faithfully for climate justice and environmental well-being. As a bond between people, *jeong* is a love that keeps people together even amid pain and suffering. Often feeling like the unconditional bond between friends and family, solidarity emerges in the sticky love of *jeong*. Connected to one another and to God, through the Spirit, we can resist the ways that our current economic and social structures

---

[22] Grace Ji-Sun Kim, *Invisible* (Minneapolis: Fortress Press, 2011), 144.

[23] Kim, 144, 145.

depend on separating each of us as individual consumers, individual actors, individual sufferers. We cannot live alone; we require *jeong* to help us love and be loved. We cannot separate ourselves from God, as God is within us and among us, and the Spirit of God draws us to live in peace with one another, encourages us to love our neighbor, and provokes us to reach out in love to others.[24]

Jeong anchors communities, churches, families, and friends by cultivating a relational framework of loyalty, devotion, and love, particularly among those who have been disenfranchised and separated. All of creation needs love and *jeong*. This sense of attachment, connection, and sticky love provokes us to loving all of God's creation. If we carry the love and build up the *jeong* with all of creation, we can really work toward sustainability. We can live into the active love of God that is present in our lives as *jeong*, between us and all of God's creation. *Jeong*, this sticky love, evokes the compassion and justice of the "kin-dom" of God. Oftentimes we philosophize God's love for us, and it all appears abstract. *Jeong* concretizes and actualizes love, casting no one away and making no one invisible.[25] All are called into the "kin-dom" of God through the dynamic, loving Spirit who blows creative Life in our midst.

God the Loving, Dynamic Spirit

The emphasis on verbs in our God-talk can best be understood and practiced in how we talk about the Spirit of

---

[24] Kim, 145, 146.
[25] Kim, 145, 146.

God. For many Christians, biblical metaphors for the Spirit evoke feelings of faithful and dynamic presence, both intimate and transcendent in our lives, and always meaningful for our well-being and flourishing. The Spirit's relationship with Mary, the mother of God, is a beautiful opportunity for us to consider the loving intimacy and dynamic, lifegiving presence of the Spirit in our own lives.

Patriarchal and status-focused readings of the relationship between the Spirit and Mary emphasize the power of the Holy Spirit to overtake and overshadow Mary. In these readings Jesus is conceived through the omnipotent power of God the Holy Spirit. Our shift to think about God's dynamic, loving Be-ing also shifts our perspective on Mary and the Holy Spirit. Loving is never coercive. Creating Spirit loves by breathing life in and for the world, and we must respond in faithful creativity for that life to flourish. Mary is not a passive recipient of a power that wants to conceive. Mary acts. Mary consents. Mary participates in the Spirit's lifegiving presence in Jesus in the conception, throughout her pregnancy, in his childhood, during his ministry, at his cross, and even after his resurrection. At different times in Christian history the Spirit has been presented as mothering, nurturing, caring, and sustaining, as a mother would be to her child.[26] Mary, the mother of God, shows us how deeply meaningful the feminine imagery of the Spirit as a mother bird brooding over her chicks can become, for it is a metaphor of active mutuality between God and the world. This imagery is helpful to many who are seeking different understandings of God that move us away from the traditional masculine and patriarchal images of God.

---

[26] Johnson, *Come, Have Breakfast*, 208, 209.

The Spirit has been described as wind, breath, and even vibration.[27] In our theological attention to verbs, we can shift these Spirit metaphors to emphasize action in our world and lives. Blowing, breathing, and vibrating are refreshing theological metaphors. These words challenge us to be attentive to and reflect upon God's movement throughout the world, as lifegiving as the precious process of breathing and as connecting as the winds that touch us all. The subtle shift to these verbs reveals the enlivening presence of the same God who says, "I Am Who I Am," who claims the mystery of activity, for our world today.

When we say God is Spirit, we are claiming that God's Be-ing inspires, literally breathes in and into us. God acts and moves with us, in us, and among us. God is. God is with us for the poor, the marginalized, the distraught, and the oppressed. God is with us for the life of creation and the whole earth. God is with us when we are lonely, distraught, broken, and sick. God is with us when we are free and when we are imprisoned. God is always with us, in our midst, in our presence, and in our lives.

Blowing Spirit

The same Creating Spirit who hovered over the waters of Genesis motivates people to act in the face of oppression. We become active co-participants in liberating and saving each other and the planet. We don't resign ourselves to our situations, but the God who is a verb shakes us up to do the work of God. When we talk about building the reign

---

[27] Grace Ji-Sun Kim, *Reimagining God: Wind, Breath and Vibration* (Eugene, OR: Cascade, 2019).

of God, we are talking about participating in doing God's work here on Earth.

When the Israelites were enslaved, God heard their cries and acted to deliver them, inspiring Moses to confront Pharaoh. In their exodus from Egypt the Israelites felt God among them as the strong wind blowing in the desert and when they were crossing the Red Sea. God was not off in some distant corner of heaven, waiting for the Israelites to die after being led out of Egypt. At the shore of the Red Sea, Blowing Spirit God made a way out of no way, liberating the refugee Israelites from their militant pursuers with a strong gust of wind. Roaming around the desert for forty years, the Israelites knew blowing wind as the presence of God, who delivered them from Egypt and would not abandon them in the desert. Blowing Spirit was a sign of God's claim that they were God's and God was theirs, with them and protecting them.

Generations later the followers of Jesus encountered Blowing Spirit during the celebration of Pentecost, remembering when God gave Torah to Moses and the desert-wandering Israelites. Blowing Spirit empowered the followers of Jesus who were gathered together to bear witness to Jews "from every nation under heaven" (Acts 2:5). Amid the confusion of the international crowd, Peter proclaimed that the God of the prophets and of David was the same God who had raised Jesus up, freeing him from death, and had poured out the Holy Spirit on the entire house of Israel (Acts 2:24, 33, 36).

Refreshing, liberating, and inspiring, God participates in our lives and frees us from our oppressions and bondages even today. Like the sending wind, which disperses seeds, spores, and pollen to perpetuate and propagate new life,

Blowing Spirit commissions us to loving justice for the life of the world. The Spirit of God is the wind who comes into our lives, changes us, and sustains us for the work of our calling. When we recognize how the Spirit of God exists in all living things, giving us life, molding us, motivating us, changing us, and giving us strength to change the world, we can engage in an eco-spiritual *metanoia* from our environmental sins. Ever the Giver of Life, Blowing Spirit God quickens life in all of creation and bids us to recognize the Spirit of God in our kindred creatures. We are called to participate in God's actions within the world, becoming co-conspirators for justice for all of creation.

Breathing Spirit

As human beings we only are alive if we can breathe. The breath of God enters us and gives us life. Without the breath of God, nothing is alive. We need the breath of God to move us and motivate us to do good in the world.

As we inhale and exhale, God's breath is moving within us. It forms us, keeps us, and sustains us. The breath of God moves throughout the universe, revealing the work of God, who creates mystery, beauty, and awesomeness in all of creation.

If you go to Hawai'i, people greet you by saying, "Aloha," which literally means, "sharing the breath of God with you." So, when you meet someone, you are sharing the breath of God, which is the Spirit of God. It is the most beautiful way to greet one another, as one acknowledges the divine within and among each other. The Spirit moves between people and connects us to one another.

As we recognize the breath of God in all things, we want to work for justice, especially justice for God's creation.

More than a politics of recognition, we seek to become co-conspirators with God for the well-being and flourishing of all creatures. *Conspiring* literally means "to breathe together," just as *inspiring* means "to become a dwelling of the Spirit." Environmental justice work is spiritual breathing together with God and others for the life of the world.

Vibrating Spirit

Vibrating may seem like an odd metaphor for God as Spirit. When we approach the world and God with an emphasis on nouns and status, it is much easier for us to assume that the status quo is how it has always been. Structures in society and the church look unchanged and unchangeable. Even the world can seem to be just a big stage upon which we act out our individual little lives. Yet, as we learn more from the natural sciences and return to the beautiful truths of the arts, we know that the whole cosmos vibrates and moves, quivering in an interconnected web of creation, motivating us to work for change, even if seemingly microscopic in its impact.

In creation stories in Genesis and John, God creates the world through God's word, through vibrating sounds that affect life in love. Every particle of the cosmos vibrates, echoing Vibrating Spirit's creativity in its own way and context. Atoms too small for unaided human sight are vibrating constantly, undermining Western philosophical and theological priorities for status and fixed order. Nothing is static when we actually participate in Vibrating Spirit's life among and within us.

When we think of the biblical creation stories, the first thing that God creates through God's word is light. Even light vibrates. Rays vibrate, giving off light so that we can see, so that photosynthesizing creatures can feed, beautifying the world across a wild spectrum of creaturely perception and sensation. As God creates the world through God's word, words form life. Vibrating creates and sustains life even if we humans have not been faithful caregivers of our thrumming, buzzing, singing world. Life means moving, vibrating, and changing in response to and relationship with the God who moves through the universe, constantly creating and transforming new life.

God Is Chi

Loving, dynamic, inspiring, breathing, blowing, and vibrating, the Spirit of God enlivens our solidarity with one another in our struggle for environmental justice as faithful disciples of Christ. As we continue to explore the theological value of verbs in our reflections on Spirit, Asian cultural understandings of the Spirit in all living things, *Chi*, can be helpful. *Chi* means breath, air, spirit, life energy, life force, wind, and breath. The concept of *Chi* is similar to *ruach* in the Old Testament and *pneuma* in the New Testament, and all three terms embody the same understanding of Spirit. The Asian concept of *Chi* portrays an embodied understanding of the Spirit; not something out there but within each of us. An embodied understanding of the Spirit challenges us to work for justice, especially intersectional environmental justice, as the Spirit is within all living things.

One of the earliest depictions of *Chi* in Chinese characters is a bowl of rice with steam arising from the bowl. This character is significant, as rice is essential for life in Asia. Rice is part of one's daily meal, and it sustains and nourishes the people. In the same way, *Chi* provides life and sustains us, filling us with energy and life. Once *Chi* leaves our bodies, we are no longer alive. Asians have understood this simple concept and recognized its importance to all of life. *Chi* needs to flow correctly, otherwise it will cause pain in our bodies, Earth, and the universe. When we have a wrong *Chi* flow within our bodies, we may see an acupuncturist or a doctor who will align our *Chi* so it can move correctly within us and not cause physical pain. The constant movement of *Chi* reminds us how Spirit is all about movement and how Spirit is in all living beings.

Chi is in the trees, the air, water, animals, and humanity. God's Spirit resides in all beings yet is not the same as each being, reinforcing a panentheistic view of God rather than a pantheistic view. Pantheism frames the God-world relationship as an equality: God is the world and the world is God. *Panentheism*, literally meaning "all in God," frames the God-world relationship with attention to the mutuality and interconnection of God and the world. As all creatures are in God, so too is God in all creatures. Spirit as *Chi* contributes to this panentheistic view to our struggle for environmental justice, tracing the shared threads of Divine Life through us all. We must treat all creatures with kindness and love, for they are bearers of the presence of God. Furthermore, how we live has an impact on the quality of God's life, for we live within God. Talking about the Spirit as *Chi* also helps us recognize that the Spirit gives us life and gives it abundantly, empowering us to change in response to new needs for flourishing and well-being in the world. As followers of Jesus, we cannot ignore the Spirit or *Chi* that exists in us and all living things. We must allow this *Chi* to move us and empower us to work for justice, equality, and sustainability.

Dove and Spirit

In Christian imagery the dove has come to represent the Spirit of God. The descent of the dove from the sky has come to signify a divine blessing "coming down" to Earth from heaven above, bringing new life. This connection between God's Spirit and the dove is shown in Jesus's baptism as the grace of new beginnings for Jesus's ministry. As Jesus came out of the Jordan River's water, heaven opened "and the Spirit descended upon him in bodily form like a dove" (Lk 3:22). At Jesus's baptism the dove signaled divine blessing upon Jesus and inaugurated his ministry to the lonely, marginalized, oppressed, and suffering world.[28]

The spiritual significance of the dove is not unique to Christianity. In Near Eastern religions the dove is treated as a representative of a female deity. Doves were tended to in cultic towers and sculpted into small clay shrines for devotees who came to worship. They symbolized the attributes of love, beauty, and fecundity associated with female deities such as the Greek goddess Aphrodite. The dove becomes a beautiful image of life, love, and the feminine, which can open us to recognize the grace of beauty and mercy upon humanity.

During the first Pentecost the Spirit of God came upon all the disciples as a rushing wind and tongues of fire (Acts 2:2–3). Even though there is no mention of a dove in the scriptural telling of that Pentecost, many artists have

---

[28] Johnson, *Come, Have Breakfast*, 206, 207.

depicted Pentecost with a dove, taking wing on Blowing Spirit's activity among the disciples. The dove is associated with the free-moving Spirit, which is gracious and merciful to all humanity.[29] The dove symbolizes grace and mercy, which we desperately need if we are going to move toward meaningful environmental justice. The dove, moving, fluttering, and hovering over us, can become a symbol of God's inspiring and protecting presence in our struggle for justice. The warmth of the mother's body supports the development of the chicks so they can hatch into new life.[30] Like Creating Spirit in the first story of Genesis, the dove can encourage our creative work amid the watery chaos of our day and can strengthen our solidarity with patient brooding over our efforts as the life-promising eggs of their young. This image of the Spirit hovering over the waters can be connected to the mother bird and provides the analogy of the creative Spirit of God, which brings forth life. The Spirit is movement, and it moves to spring forth new life into the world.

Wisdom

Finally, we must retrieve, remember, and utilize the liberative feminine image of God as Wisdom/Sophia in our theology, liturgy, and hymns as we work for climate justice. Wisdom has often been dismissed or ignored by the church with a preference for Logos over Wisdom. In the Greek and Hebrew, Wisdom is a feminine noun and name. In our current struggle for environmental well-being, the beautiful feminine images of God that Wisdom evokes can

---

[29] Johnson, 207.
[30] Johnson, 208.

help us heal from the damage done to women, particularly women of color.

Wisdom is often personified as a woman in different books of the Hebrew Bible. The books of Proverbs, Job, Ecclesiastes, Sirach, and the Wisdom of Solomon are interested in the fundamental human attributes and their relationship to the divine. Wisdom in Proverbs and the Wisdom of Solomon are personified as a woman and are often known as Woman Wisdom. "In Hebrew, *wisdom* is a grammatically feminine noun." Also, "reflections of traditional women's roles—especially aspects of the role of wife—may be seen in the characterizations of Woman Wisdom in Proverbs 3:13–18, 4:5–9, 7:4–5, and 9:1–6."[31] This feminization of Wisdom has been something that women scholars have embraced for some time. It reveals the feminine side of God, whose mothering, loving, and womanly living are important acts to reveal more of God's fullness in our relationships.

Even as a noun, Woman Wisdom unsettles theological systems that depend on the patriarchal value of a fixed status. Birthing, nurturing, accompanying, creating, vivifying, Woman Wisdom can reorient our theological thinking to the moving, acting, and becoming God. She can heighten our experience and anticipation of a God who happens, who was, is, and is to come. She can draw us to one another in a holy solidarity that prioritizes the lifegiving Breathing Spirit for all of creation. She can reveal that we, together, journey with God to become the fullness, the flourishing world. She can sound our highest call.

---

[31] Claudia V. Camp, "Woman Wisdom: Bible," *Shalvi/Hyman Encyclopedia of Jewish Women,* February 27, 2009. Jewish Women's Archive.

Discussion Questions

- How did you view or understand God in your childhood, your teenaged years, your young adulthood, and today?
- Has your understanding of God changed over time? Please reflect on how your understanding of God has been modified according to your life stages.
- What are some verbs that you think are helpful in your relationship with God? Please discuss and think of other ways that God is a verb in your own life.

5

Living with Hope

In Korea, Chuseok, the harvest moon festival, is a time when family and friends gather together to eat, make rice cakes, play games, and celebrate the harvest. Growing up as a child of an immigrant in Canada, we did not celebrate Chuseok in the full grandeur and spectacular fashion as we would have if we lived in Korea. But the small, fond memories that I have of Chuseok include my mother making Korean rice cake, called songpyeon, for us to eat during Chuseok. Songpyeon is in the shape of a small half-moon with a smooth, sticky, chewy outside cover and is filled with sweet brown sugar or sesame seeds and syrup. It is one of my favorite Korean rice cakes, and I crave it whenever we celebrate a Korean festival. Koreans love chewy food, whether noodles, bread, or rice, and we love chewy rice cakes. The chewy, soft, sweet texture is music to my mouth. As a kid, every Chuseok I waited with much anticipation as my mother spent hours in the small apartment kitchen making songpyeon, which my sister and I devoured in a matter of minutes. I could not wait until my mom made more for my feasting eyes.

Chuseok reminds us to be intimately connected to the land and appreciate the gifts of the land. Indigenous people around the world show how the land is an offering, centering its sacred presence in our lives. Koreans are indigenous to the peninsula in Asia and have lived there for thousands of years. Koreans are connected and attached to the land and have tried to take good care of the land, giving thanks for the food that the earth has produced in partnership with farmers and other creatures. Traditional Korean relationships with the land are good lessons for many of us around the world as we learn how to take care of creation. Koreans have always had a keen interest in the intertwining of creation and good health, and many remain in tune with the land and the broader cosmos, following the cyclical movements of the sun, moon, and the planets. Cultivating this attention brings a lifegiving fullness that can provoke meaningful action in our own work for climate justice today.

Sin and *Han*

"Sin language" in Christian theology generally alerts us that we are going to be talking about what happens when we go against God and our neighbors. In some theological traditions, there is a heavy focus on sin as disobeying God's commandments. In others, sin is a disease of failing to love. When we sin, we create unjust suffering and terrible pain, but a lot of theology has been focused on how sin affects God and less on how it affects others, including other-than-human creatures. We have emphasized a vertical understanding of sin that both ignores the suffering of our fellow creatures and keeps God at a distance, up above us somewhere in a pure state that we may never experience. When we seek forgiveness in this framing of sin, it is hyper-individualistic and neglects how sin damages the many relationships that make up ourselves and our world. However, the truth is that we sin against others, including nature. We sin immensely against nature. As we encounter God at the intersection of climate and justice, we have to approach sin and forgiveness with a broader attention than top-down thinking if we are to ever bring about the flourishing of all creation.

There is a Korean term, *han*, that can help as we reorient our approach to sin, emphasizing this other side of sin, the sin that we inflict on one another and nature. *Han* can be translated as "unjust suffering," which is understood as an immense suffering of the heart. *Han* emerges in the lives of those sinned against in unjust systems such as patriarchy, racism, and white supremacy. *Han* is not limited to humans, as animals and all of God's creation can experience it in the wake of devastation, violence, and oppression.

When we poison Earth, its water, land, and air, our sin intertwines with a betrayal of God, who entrusted Earth to our care. As a result, we are sinning against God's creation and God's creatures, against God's body, against God, causing lasting damage. Thinking about sin and *han* can help us confront that lasting damage long after we have stopped the sinful acts. Those most affected by our environmental wastage are people who are neglected, trampled on, and disenfranchised, pushed to the wayside by the rich and the powerful. Our siblings suffer because of the greed and the waste from rich and powerful people and nations, including our own.

We must be aware of our sin—sin against God, our human siblings, and our creaturely kindred—and paying attention to *han* means that we also must be aware of the unjust suffering that is experienced by those sinned against. All of humanity is related to one another and to the creation, our common home. We humans are deeply related to all other creatures, a family and household of creation. We can become better at caring for and loving our fellow creatures by acknowledging how individual acts of sin affect their lives. This reframes sin, moving from a vertical concern for spiritual purity or divine honor and toward a holistic attention to the well-being of us all.

Understanding this idea opens us to the possibility of reentering the family relationship we already have. By realizing the connectedness of humankind to all animal life, we become aware of new possibilities for learning and maintaining concern for the flourishing of all living things. Reframing sin with attention to *han* has the potential to reconstruct our ecological worldview to become based on reciprocity and familial relatedness instead of top-down dominance. By embracing our human dependence upon the earth and our fellow creatures, we allow ourselves renewed opportunities for sustaining our planet in mutual respect and loving hope. We can find fresh prospects for food, water, and energy that prioritize our shared flourishing and the divine gift of abundant life.

Maybe most important, we have the opportunity to focus on practical actions for repentance, healing, and restoration when we pay attention to both the guilt of the sinner and the *han* of those sinned against. Harmony in our relatedness is the key to all happiness, health, and well-being, but these mean nothing if there is not practical action to respond to our destructive ways of living. So, what can we do?

First, we must recognize and acknowledge that we are causing and creating *han* in many different communities and ecosystems throughout the earth. *Han* is not the result of other animals, of natural forces, or of God's action. Humans cause *han*, cause needless suffering, in the world. And, as discussed earlier in this book, most of the environmental harm and destruction that humans wreak in our world is caused by wealthy people and nations and occurs in patriarchal and racist patterns. We must recognize that we participate in the intersecting economic, gender, and racial oppressions that cause *han* in order to take responsibility for the suffering of the earth.

Second, we must do no harm. When we find ways to decrease the suffering of others, including other creatures and our ecosystems, we must then act to alleviate the suffering. On the large scale we need to pressure organizations and corporations to divest from fossil-fuel production and use, and we need to challenge lawmakers to write, implement, and enforce environmentally just and restorative laws to save and protect the whole creation. *Han* cannot be eliminated, though, if we only focus on massive systems. Personally, we must consider each and every action we take in life, whether political, religious, economic, or cultural. This kind of self-reflection is not easy, and changing our ways when it is necessary can take a lot of time, energy, and moral commitment.

Third, we must do good. No single action in any of our lives will be enough to stop, let alone reverse, climate injustice. But no large-scale action will occur without our individual actions to make environmental justice real in our daily lives. In order to drastically change the ways we function in day-to-day living, we need to be creative. That is, we need to create alongside the Creating Spirit of God, who breathes and blows among us. If we are to live so that other humans and other-than-human creatures will not experience *han*, we will have to actively choose alternative ways of living and cohabiting on Earth that prioritize flourishing and well-being for all. When we pay attention to gifts and needs in each of our contexts, we realize that there is no "one size fits all" solution. Each of our contexts is different, and we are each blessed with different gifts to help create the good that our world needs. None of us can heal our world alone, yet our world needs each of us to join together with the lifegiving Spirit to release the *han* that Earth's creatures are experiencing under today's climate catastrophe. The deep woundedness in our hearts can be healed, and we can flourish with all creation.

Korean parents often tell their children, "*Balli, balli.*" The expression means "hurry up," with every bit of urgency. Korean children learn this word at a young age as parents remind them to hurry up and get dressed, hurry up and get on the school bus, hurry up and eat your food. In some ways Korean culture feels like a culture on the run, always in a rush to get things done. Balli, balli is deeply embedded in the culture.

At the intersection of climate and justice is *balli balli*! We must act with urgency, for the effects of climate change are causing irreparable damage to our common home, Earth, our creaturely family, and our human communities. Before Earth loses another species to extinction and habitat loss, *balli balli*! Before fossil-fuel production and emissions damage and destroy ecosystems and human communities even further, *balli balli*! Before consumptive capitalism produces more deadly waste just briefly to fulfill our greed, *balli balli*!

When we recognize, do no harm, and do good, we can get to the work that is ahead of us with a *balli-balli* spirit that aims for flourishing and leaves no one behind. Our urgency is not haphazard, not chaotic. Our urgency is inspired. The same Blowing Spirit who hovered over the waters of creation in Genesis is with us, breathing life into our action, empowering us to change this world for the well-being of all creation.

We can act quickly to divert our communities, churches, societies, and governments from our destructive ways because we have been given the gifts to be good neighbors and relatives with all creatures. God has provided us with everything that we need to live and to flourish. God created the world and called it very good. In our greed and violence we have urgently tried to get more stuff, more power, and more independence. We have misunderstood that our urgency is supposed to be a quick response to suffering as tender caregivers in an interdependent world. We have ignored the life all around us, valuing only those creatures we can commodify and exploit.

Dandelions Are Good

Many US Americans view dandelions as undesirable weeds, if they think about them at all. An entire industry exists to kill them, creating and using herbicides to get rid of them before they spread all over a lawn that is full of non-native grasses that are fed with fertilizers that are made from fossil fuels. In some parts of the world dandelions are an important food source for humans and other creatures. In other places their resiliency can mean that they are some of the only plants at their altitude or in a drought. In still others dandelions are cultivated for medicinal purposes. The roots of the dandelion are used to make tea, and dandelion leaves can be added to salads for a fresh, healthy lunch. The leaves and roots alike are added to soups as a medicinal component.

When my daughter was younger, my mother wanted to make her some dandelion soup to help her heal from a persistent skin disease. I remember my mother carefully rooting the few dandelions out of our yard. Worried about our neighbor's pesticides, she was sure to pick only the ones from the middle of the yard. She pulled them ever so carefully from the ground, knowing that the root had much of the healing nutrients that my daughter needed to boost her immune system and fight the itchiness all over her skin.

My mother's careful selection showed the interconnectedness of our soils and our health, the body of God and our own bodies. God has created and is creating a world for our flourishing, but we have been taught to ignore, exploit, or dominate the very creatures who give good gifts for our well-being. We need the land "to live," both in the sense of our own livelihood and in the sense of its own thriving. If we continue to poison and exploit land, water, and air, we will only poison and exploit our own life together.

Our world values and rewards us when we are urgent to exploit instead of urgent to enliven, and that makes it tremendously difficult to remember that God provides what we need for our life within the household of creation. We must contribute to the well-being of the whole household and be creative with God and each other, but we can neither hoard nor ignore every gift and expect everything to be well. We need to learn from the good dandelions, receive their gifts of life, and contribute to their flourishing in love.

Flourishing

Flourishing is not just about having enough for us and living well as individuals. Flourishing means building a just society so that our neighbors have enough to eat, medical care, employment, and dignity. Flourishing involves practicing sustainability in our environmental policies and actions so that the next generations will enjoy life on this good earth. As Pope Francis writes in *Laudato Si'*, "Authentic human development has a moral character. It presumes full respect for the human person, but it must also be concerned for the world around us and 'take into account the nature of each being and of its mutual connection in an ordered system' [*Centesimus Annus*]" (no. 5) The pope is urging us to not only care for one another, but the planet that we are living on. We need to be aware of all living things and understand our connectedness to these living organisms. Without the natural order we will not have water to drink, food to eat, or land on which to live. We need to be mindful and take care of everything on Earth.

Pope Francis's words return us to the intersections of injustice that we discussed earlier in the book, particularly the intersection of environmental and economic concerns. People who live in poverty groan under the weight of hardship and difficulty caused by rich people's resource-hoarding lifestyles. The earth groans from our abuse, misuse, and exploitation. The poor and the earth groan under the weight of their *han*. We have the power to prevent this enormous suffering and must do what we can to heal one another and our whole earthly home. The gospel proclaims good news for our siblings who are poor, pushed to the margins, and disenfranchised. Furthermore, the gospel proclaims that God is with us as we take care of one another, as we learn to share the abundant life that God offers us. As we create a flourishing world with God, we must move toward a communal understanding of what it means to flourish and what it means for the earth to flourish. Like vines and branches, our own personal flourishing depends on the flourishing of others, including other-than-human creatures, in relationship with a dynamic, loving God.

Loving Our Neighbors

The Gospel of Matthew tells us that near the end of his ministry Jesus said:

> Truly I tell you, just as you did it to one of the least of these who are members of my family, you did it to me. . . . Truly I tell you, just as you did not do it to one of the least of these, you did not do it to me. (Mt 25:40, 45)

Christian work for climate justice can find its blueprint here. Today, the "least of these" are also the victims of climate change. Thus, we must change our ways of greed, overconsumption, and wastefulness to protect them.

During this time of urgent climate change, we all need to listen to the groan of the winds, the trees, and the seas, and the cries of its victims. In short, the groaning of creation is a sign that creation is suffering and in pain. We need to stop this destruction and work toward sustainability. When we faithfully follow the creating, breathing, blowing, vibrating Spirit of God, we will find ourselves in solidarity with the people who have been exploited, ignored, and oppressed in the name of power. We are in this grave climate danger together, and the poor's vulnerability is our own.

Jesus expects us to act, to love our neighbors as ourselves in faithful participation in God's abundant life for the world. Theologians like Sallie McFague, Wanda Deifelt, and Randy Woodley have helped to give us language to organize our experiences and thoughts as we struggle for environmental justice. The theology is important because, as we discussed earlier, religion affects our daily lives whether we are particularly religious or not. Yet, as Pope Francis has reminded us, our theology must encourage us to act, to love and to help those who are suffering from climate injustice. We must act now, in our own contexts and with our own gifts, for there are many things to do to help heal Earth, our common home. We need to invest in ways that protect the earth and support sustainable development.[1] We need to move away from coal and other polluting resources, including industrial farming and plantation agribusiness. We need to become creative and use renewable resources for the energy that powers our homes and lives. We must become faithful

---

[1] Grace Ji-Sun Kim, "Investing in Our Children's Future: Divestment, Sustainability, and Climate Justice" *Huffington Post,* October 1, 2014.

Christians by loving one another into the flourishing beauty of God's shalom.

Peacemaking

On a Galilean hillside, Jesus said, "Blessed are the peacemakers" (Mt 5:9). To make peace on Earth, the World Council of Churches (WCC) reminds us that we need to make peace *with* the earth. Dominant cultures in our human family have said that we are the center of creation, positioning the earth and its creatures to be objects for our domination and exploitation. Atop our fictional pinnacle of creation, we are destroying our world's wealth of gifts faster than the earth can replenish itself. From such human destructiveness we have entered a period of time some are calling the Anthropocene, the era of Earth's life that is marked by abuse, violence, and destruction caused by humans. The alienation between humanity and creation has been a violent separation, and we must work toward peace in order to heal this divide.

We must make peace in the world as an intentional act for harmony with creation. Making peace with the earth and our creaturely kindred means reducing *han* from the earth. As we have discussed throughout this book, no injustice or oppression is ever experienced on its own. Injustices intersect with one another, weaving webs that trap the poor and vulnerable in the death and despair of *han* for generations. Our peacemaking must follow Jesus to the places of oppression and the people who have been oppressed throughout the world. We must recognize how our lavish lifestyles, unbridled consumption, and participation in patriarchal and racist powers violently affect the most vulnerable climates and peoples around the planet. In solidarity with them—with the widow, orphan, and stranger, to use biblical terms—we must work for economic, racial, and gender justice as peace work.

Hoping

When will we realize that the earth is our only home? We must do all that we can to contribute to its flourishing, making it better for our children and their families. The Garden of Eden is an image of pristine beauty and love that was lost to destruction of our relationships with God and one another. We need to reflect on our path and move away from a similar path of destruction and toward a path where we make care with, justice from, and loving creativity through God a priority. God called us to be tender caregivers, a relationship of loving attentiveness to the beauty, gifts, and needs that are unique to each creature. Today, it often seems we have ignored God's call.[2]

So, where do we go from here? How can we hope when it feels as though we are irrevocably spiraling toward an increasingly destructive future, full of droughts, floods, famines, storms, and death? When we reframe our God-talk through verbs instead of nouns, we can also approach familiar things like hope with a fresh perspective. We cannot hope if hope is just another thing that can be commodified, hoarded, and systematically destroyed. Instead of some static thing that the wealthy among us can hoard, hope is practiced, enacted, lived. With God and all creation,

---

[2] Grace Ji-Sun Kim and Naomi Faith Bu, "Rescuing Home: Climate Change and COP21," *Huffington Post,* December 21, 2015.

we can hope in the face of rising sea levels, escalating temperatures, and mass extinction. We can heed the call to live sustainably and peacefully with one another and with Earth to take care of all of creation in partnership with the loving Spirit of God.

Remember to whom we belong and who loves us into abundant life. Together with all of creation we are empowered by God to hope, to advocate, and to struggle for climate justice. When we reframe hope as a verb, we can recognize the value of our little steps to mend our environments, heal our relationships, and live for new life. We can also value the need to be prophetic and proclaim to the people of the world how our behaviors must change. It is not just Christians, but followers of all religions and faith traditions, who need to commit to love one another and love the earth. We must accept one another in order to make this great hope. We must work together and work hard. We must live in harmony, holding one another in our saving work with God.

Discussion Questions

- Have you experienced *han* due to unjust systems set up to cause unjust suffering? How have you tried to eliminate your *han* so that you may live a flourishing life?
- What practical acts will you take in your own lifestyle, habits, and community to help us all live more sustainably and ecologically?
- How do you live with hope in a world facing climate crisis and climate emergency? How can we share that hope with friends and family?

Conclusion

We are part of the created community of God. You and I, humans in our particular times and places, share Earth as a common home with other animals, with plants, with fungi, with water systems, and with soil microbiomes. We live in ecosystems that overlap, and our own lives are marked by intersecting identities and relationships. We are earthbound, woven within the creation through the lifegiving creativity of the Spirit of God. As we confront the devastating realities of climate change and environmental injustice, we do not do it alone. In solidarity with God and the household of all creation, we can become a source of healing justice, transforming love, and flourishing creativity.

In this book we have considered how our current climate changes are causing environmental catastrophes, including severe storms, droughts, soil erosion and degradation, water pollution, water shortages, air pollution, and the migration and extinction of animals. These disruptions irreparably change ecosystems that have supported thriving communities of life that included humans for millennia. These changes are caused by human activity, particularly the industrial and capitalist activity that commodifies the good gifts of creation, exploits our fellow creatures as resources, and creates dangerous emissions by burning fossil fuels for seemingly inexpensive and endless energy.

Over centuries of colonialism, white colonizers and settlers have taken Indigenous lands through both treaties and theft, carrying out genocides of the native peoples in the process. Colonialism has allowed for and encouraged large corporations to expropriate and exploit environments around the world to support unsustainable and inequitable consumption behaviors in many different societies. More than politics, economics, or ecological anthropology, we have discussed how Christian theology has influenced and been influenced by these histories and practices of domination and destruction. Most important, we have proposed real changes that we must make as people of faith to advocate for climate justice, protect the planet, live sustainably, and make peace through ecological justice work.

We cannot live oblivious to the Indigenous Peoples who describe for us the impact of our actions on creation. We cannot turn away from the reality of vanishing species among the animals with whom we share this planet. We cannot ignore Earth's painful cries in mega-storms, severe droughts, rising sea levels, melting icebergs, increasing temperatures, and deadly forest fires. We cannot continue to insist that God is some kingly CEO on high, removed from our sufferings and from the cries of the poor. We must heed the warnings all around us and address the intersecting social injustices that intensify environmental crisis and creaturely suffering alike. Our move into sustainable, loving, and creative relationships within God's creation will be nothing short of a conversion that embraces the lifegiving Spirit who fills us all.

Throughout this book we have identified how and explored why our religious commitments are tied up in our environmental relationships. Indigenous Peoples have understood environmental justice as an integral spiritual way in their particular contexts since time immemorial. The connection of environmental justice and spirituality is rooted in fundamental understandings of our interrelatedness within the sacred creation. Learning from Indigenous Peoples and ecological currents within Christian history, we can recognize that the ecological crisis is a theological crisis because it is about our relationship with our Creator, one another, and all of creation. As a theological crisis, we are confronted with the stark reality that Christian theologies have supported the environmental violence that is causing so much suffering.

Our work together for environmental justice must include rethinking and reframing our experiences of God and our commitments of faith. We cannot understand God in the same old ways, perpetuating ecological devastation and blessing greed, domination, and exploitation in our efforts to become like an all-powerful Divine Emperor. Theological metaphors are necessary and important tools that we use to try and understand our experiences of God, and it is time for new images and metaphors of God that encourage the lifegiving grace of the Holy Spirit that we read about in the creation stories.

I have said that we need to deconstruct the noun understanding of God and talk about God as a verb. By reimagining God with verbs, we can focus on God's actions in this world and God's dynamic love for this world. God's actions and the presence of God in our lives, and the world will encourage us human beings to act and act quickly to stop harming our fellow creatures and to heal the suffering that we have caused. When we recognize God's movement within, through, and all around us, we reframe our relationships with other creatures because we recognize that the Spirit of God lives and breathes through them too. We can recognize how our sins against air, water, plants, and animals hurt God too. This is a radical shift in how Western Christian societies have understood the relationship between body and spirit. The Spirit of wind, breath, light, and energy gives us all the courage, strength, and love to work for climate justice in a broken world.

Many human cultures remind us that the Spirit exists within all things, and Christian environmental action must learn how to experience the Spirit as it is embodied in other creatures. This spirit is understood in different ways in different cultures. In Asian cultures, we call it *Chi*, and we believe that *Chi* resides in all living things as the spirit of life, giving life to all living things. When we shift our theological attention to verbs, Christians can embrace a belief that the Spirit who hovers over the waters of creation also dwells in all living things, and we can change how we live to become more loving caregivers of God's creation.

For too long Christians have rejected this idea in favor of a dualistic split between spirit and body, or between spirit and the natural world. In different traditions this divide has infected Christian understandings of, teachings about, and actions toward real human and creaturely bodies. Without ever witnessing the interconnectedness of the Spirit with the world, we have sanctioned tremendous violence against each other, our fellow creatures, and the Holy Spirit itself. Western Christians have been able to justify exploiting and killing people under colonial, imperial, and industrial systems by separating the Spirit from the world and denigrating the integrated spiritualities of paganism, shamanism, and ancestor worship that were practiced by many Asian, African, and Indigenous Peoples around the globe. Our separation of the spirit and the body is neither faithfully Christian nor is it good for the earth. When we have failed to see how the Spirit moves in our lives and connects us with other creatures and the whole earth, we have failed to become good stewards to and tender caregivers of God's creation.

Clearly, we earthbound creatures have work to do. Some of us need to repent and practice *metanoia*, turning away from negative understandings of the spirit and our bodies, from sins of overconsumption and greed, or from the tempting power of patriarchal control and domination. Others of us need to heal, for we have experienced generations of *han* from the intersecting injustices of poverty, racism, sexism, and the like. All of us need to be "in-spired," to be breathed into by the God whose Be-ing among us is a gift of abundant life.

Together, we can be connected with land and Spirit as a genuine community of creation. We can meet God at the intersection of climate and justice. We can reevaluate the rules of the household so that we can respect one another and commit to the flourishing of all of creation. We can embrace theologies that empower healing, solidarity, and liberation. We can hope together, making a world of greater peace a reality in our lives. We can be transformed in the lifegiving adventure of the Spirit, who creates with and among us. With God and all of creation, we must make it so.